P9-DFQ-984

HOW TO
**HAVE A
48-HOUR
DAY**

How to Have a 48-Hour Day

Copyright © 1996 by Don Aslett.

Printed and bound in the United States of America. All rights reserved. No part of this book may be reproduced in any form or by any electronic or mechanical means including information storage and retrieval systems without permission in writing from the publisher, except by a reviewer, who may quote brief passages in a review.

Published by Marsh Creek Press, PO Box 700, Pocatello, Idaho 83204 1-208-232-3535.

MARSH CREEK PRESS

Distributed by Betterway Books, an imprint of F&W Publications, Inc., 1507 Dana Avenue, Cincinnati, OH 45207. 1-800-289-0963.

ISBN 0-937750-13-1

Illustrator: Val Chadwick Bagley
Designer: Craig LaGory
Editor: Carol Cartaino
Production Manager: Tobi Haynes

"Checklist for Action" p. 110 copyright Carol Cartaino and Howard I. Wells.

Library of Congress Cataloging-in-Publication Data

Aslett, Don, 1935-
　　How to have a 48-hour day / Don Aslett ; illustrated by Val Chadwick Bagley.
　　　　p.　cm.
　　ISBN 0-937750-13-1 (pbk.)

　　1. Time management. 2. Life skills. I. Title.

HD69.T54A85　1996
640'.43--dc20

95-49880
CIP

ALSO BY DON ASLETT

Business Books:

The Office Clutter Cure

How to be #1 With Your Boss

Everything I Needed to Know About Business
I Learned in the Barnyard

Speak Up!

Help for Packrats:

Clutter's Last Stand

Not for Packrats Only

Clutter Free! Finally & Forever

How to Clean / Professional Cleaning Books:

Is There Life After Housework?

Do I Dust or Vacuum First?

Make Your House Do the Housework

Don Aslett's Clean in a Minute

Who Says It's a Woman's Job to Clean?

500 Terrific Ideas for Cleaning Everything

Pet Clean-Up Made Easy

How Do I Clean the Moosehead?

Don Aslett's Stainbuster's Bible

The Cleaning Encyclopedia

Cleaning Up for a Living

The Professional Cleaner's Personal Handbook

How to Upgrade & Motivate Your Cleaning Crews

Painting Without Fainting

TABLE OF CONTENTS

P R E F A C E

After you've heard the same basic statement 40 or 400 (or even 4000) times, you realize it deserves some attention. One day it occurred to me how often people come out with remarks related to time and "doing," and I started jotting them down:

"Doesn't seem like I got much done today."

"Good grief, where did all the time go?"

"It couldn't be noon already, I just got started."

"I didn't do half what I intended this week."

"I've got enough scheduled for two lifetimes."

"If I could just skip sleeping, I might catch up."

"If only I had more time."

"What I need is a 48-hour day!"

We've all said things like this and heard them over and over from others in every type of situation—home, work, play, and business. But that last one, "What I need is a 48-hour day," intrigued me, because that little comment sums up all the others:

WHAT I NEED IS MORE TIME!

Haven't we all attacked the time problem with every new approach and technique around, yet the outcome is that **we still don't have enough time**, or at least as much as we want. We all have a thousand things more to do than we're doing now, if we just had the time.

So we "timeless" complainers have attempted in vain to stretch time, buy time,

save time, stop time, find time, and beat time. We are even foolish enough to think we can manage time. You don't and won't do any of these and you don't make time either (wow, what a commodity if you could manufacture time and sell it!).

We have only one alternative here, there is only one single thing we can do with time and that is **use it**. We can't manage time but we can manage our own behavior and activities to use it wisely.

The person who wanted the 48-hour day gives us a starting place, a reason for this book. We'd all like to double our output in life, get 48 hours' worth out of the 24. I meet thousands of people every year in my seminars, presentations, and media appearances, and no matter where I am, what the purpose of the assemblage, or what the assigned topic, the thing I'm most often asked is **"Gosh, Don, how do you get so much done?"**

The answers in this book are my answers, not a compilation of what two dozen other "how to beat the clock" books out there have to say. This is not the usual collection of sanctified information from Harvard or Yale, or the findings of fifty research assistants. I don't have secret formulas, a four-pound organization and scheduling workbook, or any chants or prayers to transform you into a more efficient functioner in life. And I don't know all the answers. But I do have a proven track record and I know from an ordinary, everyday standpoint how to get more done, how to do a thousand things at once, how to have 48-hour days. I can help you produce much more than you are now and make you more valuable to yourself and others, hence more **needed** and **loved**.

Is there anything we want more than that?

Don Aslett

Doing more, being a go-getter, doesn't mean just making more money or scoring more points. It applies to not just "work" and business but every aspect of life—family, community, church, and social activities, arts, athletics. If we do more and better in anything we will benefit. We all know that, and that's why everyone wants to know "How can I get more done?"

CHAPTER ONE

Why Do More?

Taking a stand or even making a statement that involves rating people or establishing qualifications for anything is downright risky in these days of "equality" of jobs, sexes, and rights. But let's risk it! Let's point out a gross inequality in the human condition.

Just or not, like it or not, there seems to be a pretty clear ranking of people according basically to **how much they can get done**. Doing draws a dividing line quicker and surer than any separation you'll ever see. And the doers, those 48-hour day people, have an advantage, a deserved advantage, over the regular run of humankind. Most of this you've witnessed, much of it you've even said, and here are the ABC's of it:

A. The **go-getters** and the **do-morers** are the people most desired and admired, it's that simple.

B. The world rewards them the most, bosses hire and pay them the most, the Lord loves them the most (that's scripture!), and they even seem to have the most fun.

C. Average people get treated average, the high producers, the doers, get treated the best, and it's only fair and logical that they should. Those who do the most **should** get the most.

If you have any doubts about this, since we believe in the democratic system, let's vote on it!

The following are some of the main reasons for doing more. If you agree with each of these and/or would like to have that advantage, vote yes. If not, check no. Whether you wear a 48-hour day watch or just want one (or are even jealous of those who do), vote honestly.

Official Ballot:

Why get more done?

Yes ☐ No ☐ WHY DO MORE?

To find genuine **self-respect**. We always know, deep down, whether we're accomplishing anything or not. And no external pleasure can beat the inner satisfaction of knowing we can do it, that we DID it!

Yes ☐ No ☐ WHY DO MORE?

To avoid passenger status. Doing more will put you in the driver's seat, so you can get behind the wheel and go where and when you want to go. The average achiever has to generally be content to be hauled wherever others want to take him.

Yes ☐ No ☐ WHY DO MORE?

For a better job. **Production** is what every employer is looking for. Production is valuable and people who produce are promoted and well paid as well as praised.

Yes ☐ No ☐ WHY DO MORE?

So you *qualify*. Notice how for many things in life—a license, a loan, a policy, a school, a team, a race, or a mortgage, we have to qualify before we are accepted. We humans, in a more subtle way, do exactly the same thing with each other—we qualify people before we decide to hire, love, or want them. If you don't measure up, you don't get the mate or the mortgage or whatever. If you've wandered through life for years wondering what was wrong, **why you never seem to get the breaks**, it may well be because of your output.

Yes ☐ No ☐ WHY DO MORE?

For family strength! For a better marriage. Many divorces are a result of the fact that one of the parties is a non-producer. They don't produce a living, a pleasing personality, a clean home, an example for the kids, a feeling of companionship and appreciation, etc.

"Average" always ties a slip knot.

Yes ☐ No ☐ WHY DO MORE?

To have more choices and not be left to chance as much.

Yes ☐ No ☐ WHY DO MORE?

High production is also a great communicator. Many things are misunderstood because they were written or said wrong, but actions come across clearly. When something is done (not planned, promised, or intended, **but DONE**), little has to be said or explained or evaluated—the act speaks for itself. The more good works you do, the less you have to preach! In fact, they shouldn't allow sermons, there should just be a **report** on what acts of charity have been done that week—that would give all the message and inspiration needed.

Yes ☐ No ☐ WHY DO MORE?

Because a day will come when you'll **have** to do more, you'll have no choice as to whether or not you want to, you'll have to... and will you know how? When you face a financial bind or stepped-up competition in your business or profession, when you're suddenly in charge of a company, a church, or a family... or you have two sets of twins. If you know how to do more, you'll handle it well and even enjoy it; if you don't, you'll experience frustration, disappointment, and failure rather than rewards.

Yes ☐ No ☐ WHY DO MORE?

For attention, all-eyes-on-you attention! Average may get an honorable mention, but producers get our full attention. It's the doer, the leader, the inventor, the explorer, that we all want to hear about.

Talents and virtues are of little value if they aren't used and recognized. If you do a lot, you'll have an unmistakable identity: What you do is who you are.

Yes ☐ No ☐ WHY DO MORE?

To have influence. Because you become a number setter instead of just a number, you count instead of being counted. You matter, instead of just being matter. You make a difference in life and society. We quickly lose interest in people who don't contribute. People not only love producers, they listen to them.

If we were only allowed a one-word epitaph, I'd want mine to be "productive." Generous, kind, rich, and reverent are nice, too, but all of the above are easily or potentially included in productive.

Yes ☐ No ☐ WHY DO MORE?

Leverage! We so often use the wrong tools to get our way, to influence others, to get a raise, a transfer, a sale—we try politics, unions, payoffs, begging, bullying, and forty other inferior approaches, all taking time and effort and resulting in a doubtful outcome. Higher production is the greatest leverage in the world. Real producers can name their price and place and write their own tickets. If you're a poor or average doer, you go where you're told, and for what you're offered. If you're a real producer, you go where and when you want and for the price you have in mind.

Yes ☐ No ☐ WHY DO MORE?

For that elusive thing called **security**. I love General Douglas MacArthur's definition of security: *The ability to produce.* As long as you can and do produce, you have a certain security. Job security, for example, is a darn good reason to do more. You don't want to be one of those thinned from the ranks when the thinning starts. Few key people, go-getters, producers get thrown away or weeded out. Few bosses or company owners will let a productive person go. Titles and positions are only temporary, but solid output or production lasts and lasts.

Yes ☐ No ☐ WHY DO MORE?

So that you will expand as you grow older, not diminish. So many people spend all their time looking forward to retirement, to **withdrawal** from production. But age seasons us into, not out of, our best productive years. When we're older we have more to give and teach, we're more qualified to guide, direct, and advise. If you want an exciting life, you have to keep putting out the effort to do exciting things, until you're 95 or 105! If you retire from production, everyone (except those who are after your money) will gradually retire from you.

Yes ☐ No ☐ WHY DO MORE?

For the carryover—it will aid and improve every area of your life! Once you get down the principles of getting lots done in one area, the same laws and like principles usually apply to other situations. We've all noticed how people who become superior in one thing seem to somehow have a golden touch for other things. That is carryover.

Yes ☐ No ☐ WHY DO MORE?

For the financial rewards. People who do more get more in the long run, they profit economically as well as physically and emotionally. There is a tough, but true lesson most of us have learned by now— we aren't rewarded for just wandering around in life. Those who do more, get more—it's the law of the harvest and the law of the jungle, the work ethic and the religious ethic.

Yes ☐ No ☐ WHY DO MORE?

Productive people are almost irresistible—they attract others and draw respect, help, cooperation, and opportunities from all sides. Their very presence creates energy that draws the good deals.

Think for a minute of the things, people, and events that impact and influence you the most. Anything or anyone that produces, we have a natural love for. The dolphin at Sea World that just swims

DO YOU THINK I'M MEDIOCRE?

ALMOST.

around and makes or fakes a feeble jump for fish is "ho-hum," but the one who throws his whole life into his leaps, we love him. We love the car that goes the fastest, the garden soil and fruit trees that yield the most and best. It's the doer we all love, because working hard and producing a lot brings out all of the knowledge and passion in a person.

Yes ☐ No ☐ WHY DO MORE?

To give yourself a real sense of purpose. The do-too-muchers are always happier and less depressed than the never-do-enoughers. Knowing you are doing something that matters is a big, if not **THE** biggest motivating factor in the world.

Yes ☐ No ☐ WHY DO MORE?

To cut waste. People who spend more time achieving don't have the time, space, or desire to stockpile "junk" or useless things. When you're doing more you don't have time to do the slippage things, either... no time for excess spending, gossiping, or hurting people's feelings. Even sinning gets harder to work into your schedule.

Yes ☐ No ☐ WHY DO MORE?

You'll at last be able to keep your output up with your imagination! Think of that.

Yes ☐ No ☐ WHY DO MORE?

It's only right! Our existence takes up space, wears things out, we use up food and energy and public roads and buildings, etc. Helping, doing our share to re-

place, replenish, and rebuild things is an obligation we all have. It's our duty to produce a lot!

Yes ☐ No ☐ WHY DO MORE?

It takes you out of average. Neither you nor anyone else really wants or seeks out the average, the ordinary. Do you go fishing for the smallest fish? Want to read the average book or see the average movie? Do you want an average spouse, an average job, average health? Do you say at payday, "Oh, just give me the average?" Do you want an ordinary or average vacation, vehicle, or dinner?

It's human nature to want to excel, and to love those who excel. There isn't one pursuit of life, office to university, ballfield to ballroom, where people don't want and expect **the best.** All of our improvement, progress, growth, education, knowledge, striving, sacrifice... is all for what? To be better, to do more. Average isn't bad, it's just less recognized and rewarded. Doing more will put you past average.

If you voted YES on eleven or more of these reasons to do more, then you have good reason to read on, to win and wear a 48-hour watch!

WHY DO MORE, IN SHORT

Let me sum up this production business now with the bottom line of life, which is basically two things—to love and be loved. If you can achieve these two things, the other 10,000 needs and wants will follow by themselves.

It feels SO good to be loved and needed. Being cared about is the greatest pleasure and experience on the face of the earth. It never gets old, we can't have too much of it. What does it really take to be loved? **Production**! We pity, tend, and tolerate depressed, tired, "ordinary effort" people—we don't love them.

As for that equally important business of lov*ing*, what other measuring stick is there for it if not what and how much we do? Looks? Talk? Position? Money in the bank? Promises? Intentions? We can have all of these and still be worthless and undesirable. Love is **doing**, not feeling.

PRODUCTION ISN'T JUST MECHANICAL OUTPUT

Don't confuse **more time** with more stuff or more status. A 48-hour day is "to do," not "to get," for what you can accomplish and become, not just what you can have.

When you hear the word production, don't just think of assembly lines or the factories downtown. That's just mechanical output. Production can be bigger, better, greater accomplishment in anything.

- Teaching lessons, in the classroom or anywhere, that change lives
- Preparing quality meals
- Playing music that will lift and touch others
- Creating a pleasant and beautiful yard or garden
- Displaying determination and drive that inspires others
- Caring for children, the aged, or anyone well, making them comfortable and safe and happy, is one of the most productive things on earth.

Getting a lot done doesn't exclude the things that just give you enjoyment like knitting, fishing, or taking pictures, either.

Production isn't always tangible, but it does always result in a recognizable change in something. A talk, poem, or deed that changes attitudes or behavior—lives—is wonderful production. Some very tangible results will usually follow on their own.

WHY HAVE A 48-HOUR DAY?

Why do more? It's the most direct route to what we're all looking for.

It's the answer to most of our problems. It gives us self-esteem, satisfaction, and a sense of purpose, as well as a good livelihood. Production keeps us in touch, in focus, in demand, in charge, and interesting (not to mention, **in income**!). Production generates more self-worth, security, and personal value, than any other single alternative.

So let's do something! Lots!

Ordinary Me, Do More?

Every book needs a "Little Engine That Could" chapter, and this is it. An answer to that question that's forming in your mind right now, "But can plain old ordinary me do more?"

Too many people believe that they have to be or know some kind of efficiency expert to be able to use time better. They're convinced you have to attend a seminar, gain a college degree, lug around a thick calendar planner, or get the right kind of computer program to master the magic of MORE... absolutely not true!

There are those out there trying to make a mystery out of time efficiency. It's not a mystery, nor is it difficult—and your time IQ is equal to anyone's, whether you're a bank clerk from Boston, secretary from St. Louis, phone repairman from Phoenix, or babysitter in Sioux City. When it comes to the opportunity to do more, a Montana ranch hand is on equal footing with a Madison Avenue executive. Most mothers can "out efficiency" professors of productivity at major universities.... And YOU— I don't care what your age, sex, location, education, size, color, or creed may be— have exactly the advantages and disadvantages when it comes to time use that the people with the big names and numbers have. The clock runs the same for all of us—plain old everyday people, or rich, powerful, famous ones. You have the knowledge, desire, and whispering of the spirit that you can do **more and better,** so now get rid of the "time scholar stigma," the idea that high producers are some kind of extraordinary other guy out there.

I meet thousands of people who because they "ain't schooled" think they are unqualified to be masters of doing more. And I meet thousands of others who because they are schooled (or on their way to it), think they have the inside track. Both are wrong, as far as time use and great production is concerned. So whether you worry about your lack of formal learning, or those letters you have behind your name from years of higher education are puffing you up, forget it, it has little to do with wearing a 48-hour watch. The only abbreviations that really count here are A.M. and P.M.

If you think you are ordinary, aren't we all? And you know as well as I do that any of us has the capacity to do more in life than we are doing right now. I've worked and mixed with all kinds of people from the farms of the West to the fancy studios of the world's largest TV networks and the offices of some of this country's biggest organizations and companies. I've taught in schools, run many businesses, hired over 40,000 people, authored many books, entertained and spoken to hundreds of thousands of people in the course of more than 10,000 public appearances. And I know from repeated experience that **a little "extra"** is all it takes to make a person extraordinary.

EXTRA is easy to understand and within the reach of all of us—you, me, anyone who wants it. So just add extra to ordinary and there—YOU are one of those extraordinary people you hold in awe!

WHAT IS THEIR SECRET?

What common virtue do all of the following people have, for example? They're not all physically attractive or rich, not the same race or religion, some are educated and some are not. Their likeness is a simple one... they are all doers, high producers. They always stand out because there aren't a lot of them around.

A retired farmer, 65 years old, spending his summers in a high class resort area, was hired by a contractor to do odd jobs and small repairs and construction projects. He worked with three other employees—"young college studs"—all doing the same kind of work. In a couple of months the old man was the **only employee**, and he did all the work and did it better and faster than his former three colleagues put together. What was his secret?

A young Lt. Colonel retired from the air force, and along with many of his high-ranking comrades he faced a bleak employment situation back in civilian life. While his friends looked for the best-paying jobs they could possibly find, refusing most because of their "overqualification," this fellow took a $24,000 a year job, with bonuses for bonus results. By his second year he was making $200,000 and his buddies were still struggling to find something.

The entire town in the Western mountains was in a slump. On every side were nothing but discouraged workers and vacant shops. There were no jobs, the economy was bad, nothing was selling, etc. But materials right from those very mountains and forests were shipped to Japan and made into products that were then shipped all the way back to the area. And they sold faster than the Japanese could produce them.

A 25-year-old wrestling teacher, wanting to make more money than a teacher's salary, launched into his own painting business (he'd never painted in his life). He made not only money, but friends and customers. Then he decided to become a house builder, right at the worst possible time (high interest rates, in the middle of a recession, etc.). He'd never built a thing in his life, but he moved to a likely area and hit the streets to build, with no backing or well established background. In just one year, during which many of the old experienced builders "went under," this young developer had $50,000 in profits in his pocket, had 22 new houses underway, and was designing and building his own dream house, too.

He did plenty of free, donated work for his church and community, as well.

Most of the local farmers took care of 80 to 160 acres of row crops, with the aid of a small army of border labor. A man moved into the area and cultivated and cared for 400 acres of row crops, with no hired help, just family. He made a big profit and had time to fish and hunt and enjoy himself, too.

A resort operated the same way for 38 years with the same number of people to do the maintenance—cleaning, laundry, deliveries, landscaping, etc. It took 45 people in all. A young man cleaning phone booths near the resort stopped in and talked himself into a chance to contract the work. Eventually the 45 people were replaced with 15 and the quality of the work only improved.

An industrious homemaker seemed unable to keep her head above water after she had her third child. About when she'd reached the height of frustration, a neighbor with nine children, ages two to twelve, moved next door and kept a much larger house immaculate. The new neighbor had two church jobs, played softball, made elaborate quilts in her spare time. She traveled every year, wrote and sold articles, and contracted the building of her own house! And from time to time she came over and helped her struggling neighbor.

A high intensity office of corporate executives needed top efficiency out of a secretary. So they pooled their work and one mature, adept, well educated, and well experienced woman would arrive early, bend her back over it all, and slave. She poured out the paperwork and drafts in total dedication, accomplishing a seemingly admirable amount. Then a part-time substitute, a shy farm girl with only a high school education, assumed the job and accomplished more (and more accurately) in two hours than her predecessor did in eight.

A young woman who worked in a copy center for minimum wage was admired for her hustle and accuracy by a customer and hired by that customer for "secretarial duties" in his company. Within two years, she handled all the marketing, copywriting, layout, printing, mailings, scheduling, media contacts, training others in the office on the computer, payables, receivables, and every errand around. Her accuracy and hustle only expanded with the "more."

I could tell you hundreds more stories like this, and you could tell me of as many situations where time was used better somehow, some way, by people who managed to do more—just common ordinary folks, too. There is no big secret here, it's just everyday people applying some simple old standby ideas and principles, and that little extra that makes you extraordinary.

The retired farmer came in at 7:30 a.m. and got his tools ready, and by eight o'clock was working. He didn't run, just plodded

along. But he didn't take long lunches, never stopped working to talk, never took breaks, and never fixed anything twice. He loved every minute of his work and a long list of people wanted to hire him.

The young Lt. Colonel made 200 calls per day on his clients. He was at the office at 7:00 a.m. and treated his customers like gold. His colleagues made 40 calls/contacts a day, got to work at 8:30, and once they gained an account they forgot the customer.

The discouraged workers from the vacant shops were complainers, surly, never satisfied with employment terms and conditions, and backed up by unemployment compensation and other security bumpers. Their competitors across the ocean knew only a few words: smile, hustle, and produce a quality product.

The 25-year-old teacher studied building two hours a day in the late nights or early mornings, and was on the job the rest of the time. He never used prime work time to twink, visit, or daydream.

The man who moved to the farm planned carefully and plowed even when it was cold. He spent less than he took in and stayed home and worked more than he roamed the town. He didn't spend any time in bars or lounging in hot tubs or on beaches. He stayed in the field or in the barnyard where his duties were.

The new contractor at the resort didn't have a chance to learn all of the rules for avoiding work and killing time while still getting paid. He simply had his people work all the time they were on the job, and thus got the job done a lot faster as well as better.

The new neighbor had the same number of arms and legs, and was no smarter or more energetic than the struggling one. She had no special training and her children (like all children) weren't magnificently obedient. Her big secret, she said, was simply reading and following the ways to speed up cleaning in *Is There Life After Housework?* (See the order form at the back of the book.)

The shy Wyoming farm girl had nine brothers and sisters, and knew from earliest childhood not only how to shoulder a full load, but how to cheerfully help with and assume chores besides her own. She carried this habit of output with her to the office, and the work was a piece of cake for her.

The corporate superwoman who went from minimum wage to maximum output is a mother as well, an everyday American girl with a special accomplisher's attitude: "I'm at my best when overrun with work, job demands, and opportunities." The only word she ever misspells is work, she spells it f-u-n.

YES YOU CAN DO MORE

We hear "I can't find the time" or "as soon as I find some time I'll..." over and over as an excuse to stay static. Time doesn't need to be found, it is in plain sight ticking away loudly all the time. How we use it is the only question.

Consider a college student who takes on the class schedule of the average four-year course of study. Most students think they are suffering and sacrificing to get through this, and when carrying a "full load" figure they are about "maxed out." During my six years in college and in the years since, I've had a chance to observe

students of all ages, 18-60. Some are completely busy just attending classes and cashing checks from grants, scholarships, and their folks. Others attend classes, work full time, have families, and take part in extracurricular activities. Others do even more than that. My partner Arlo, a full-time pharmacy student with four children, worked on a job ten hours a day while in college and did lots of church and community work, too. Yet he still was better ranked when he graduated than his colleagues who (supported by others) just went to class and studied all the time.

When my wife and I enrolled in school we were married and totally self-supporting. In the next five years, **while a full-time student**, I started a cleaning business and built it up to a big company that employed hundreds of students. We too not only earned our degrees but had four children during our college years, bought a house, and were active in church and community work and student government. I was also on the debate team, and played and lettered three years as a college athlete. We hunted, fished, took the kids all over, sang in choirs, etc.—all while full-time students and we still had time and could have done more. Looking back now, we view that as a pretty simple easy time.

Sure one class, course, or commitment can keep you busy and use up all your time, if that's what you want and expect and accept out of yourself. But you can do more, lots more, you can and should wear that 48-hour watch.

We've all met new mothers who have their first baby and are overwhelmed. I've had many say that the baby (just one) had them to their limit. When my wife tells

them we had six little kids in seven years, and for a time had eight teenagers living in our home at once, they stare in total disbelief. There are women out there, too, who have twelve children, yet are calm, attractive, and in control. Their kids are well mannered, their homes a pleasure to be in, they have personal lives, and they're active in church and community too, and they are just ordinary folks. All of this says **more CAN be done.**

You are a human being, capable of all kinds of incredible accomplishments and creations. Surely using time better, stacking up a few more blocks to build a better life isn't asking too much.

The biggest inhibitor of "more" is waiting for an outside force to do it for us, to drag us up by the bootstraps—the government, God, the company, or our parents. We somehow think there is someone out there somewhere in official charge of "more." Maybe an agency with a budget of

48-hour-day clocks to give us when we are declared a disaster.

We may not even doubt that we can and should do more, but we need those more-makers to step into our lives and lift us up to the effort. Even if that were true, who wants to be wound up like some spring-loaded toy, then dance and flip and whirl around, race and roll all over? Then run down, stopped right where you ran out of mainspring, waiting for a rewind or someone to furnish you a new battery.

As for the "at my age" cop out, what difference does age make? We're never too young or too old to do more. For some reason we've gotten in the habit of thinking we shouldn't expect much out of the young or the old. Why not? These are some prime times of life. Young, we have energy, strength, ambition, unequalled imagination, and time, and old we have wisdom and experience. Why do we move our mature people to the upright grave-yard called retirement? It's a lot of smarts wasted. Who said you're supposed to wind down with the years?

I've known people who under terrible pressure and in impoverished conditions have cared for handicapped children in the midst of forty other jobs and responsibilities, and it only strengthened them. Seldom is there truly "**too much**" to do, most people just have other unsolved or unresolved things nagging at them, so they never dedicate their time and energy to the work.

Several years ago, when living in the Sun Valley resort area, I was called to preside over a church congregation with the authority to appoint others in the congregation to help with teaching, singing,

services, visiting the sick, helping the needy, and other jobs. When I first got there the congregation was small and yet we still needed a full staff to run all the different programs. So most of the volunteer members were doing four separate church jobs, like teaching a class on Sunday, another during the week, counseling youth and helping with church welfare efforts, etc. Those were fun and progressive days—everyone had a lot to do and did it well. They were cheerful and committed, they were needed and they knew it. They wouldn't and really couldn't miss church or one of their assignments, even if they were sick nigh unto death.

As the area and our company grew, more and more new people moved in, and soon each member only had three jobs. They didn't seem to have quite the same fire in them, or as much time for church affairs. And then more people moved in, and each member only had two jobs. They still did okay, but weren't nearly as go-getting as they'd been when they had four. Then as skiing and Sun Valley really boomed in the early 70's, we had a large congregation, so were able to function in the normal way, fully organized, each member now had **one** assignment. Now some of the real performers with four jobs before were real draggers with one, and they didn't enjoy it as much. And all the complaints now were about time shortage.

I've seen this on all types of jobs, all types of athletic teams, in the army, and in the classroom. When the demands are hard, more than normal, straining even— people will respond and be activated and inspired to do more and better than they do on a light schedule.

My company once cleaned buildings at 1,500 square feet an hour. That was shining, unbeatable, maximum time use, we thought. Then we came up against tougher big-city competition and learned to clean at 2,500 square feet an hour, beyond belief! Today we are bidding and cleaning those same buildings at 5,000-6,000 square feet an hour!

A field supervisor in the pineapple fields of Hawaii told me a similar story one afternoon. "For twenty years, workers in the fields here were planting 5,000 and 6,000 plants per day; that was what was expected and that was what was done. If someone managed 7,000, it was awesome. Then the pineapple companies began to hire 16- and 17-year-old kids for the summer and bring them to Hawaii to plant pineapples as the older workers retired and the locals didn't think they should do such work. One day a young man from Idaho, not knowing how many to plant per day, did 12,000. Now most are doing far more."

Most of us consciously or unconsciously do what is **average**, what's been done and accepted before. If one report a day is par, then one report is what is done. Then as someone is busy doing just that, a new manager walks in and says "I always get two reports a day out of my people, and that's how it will be if you want to be one of my people." He gets two reports a day, and none of the "one reporters" a day can understand what happened, they are still busy about the same.

While doing a study once for a telephone company in Chicago, I noticed that one of their top cleaners only cleaned two restrooms a day. But boy, were they clean, you almost had to shield your eyes when you walked into them. And so this fellow and his boss received constant praise—the boss (who had never gotten compliments for restrooms before) thought all was well and didn't want to rock the boat. But any janitor can clean 500 square feet of restroom per hour. I informed the boss that the person doing the great job on the two could easily, without any strain at all, do 17 more in the day just as clean. So the boss assigned 19 and that fellow is now doing 19 daily and they look just as good as those original two.

Or think about jugglers, for another example. I can juggle two items, my son can do three, and my son-in-law, four. He's twice as good as me, so I should assume he's the best, not much better can be done, right? We realize how ridiculous that is when we see someone juggle ten things. Ten different things! With his hands or his feet! In a windstorm! Blindfolded!

Johnny Weismuller, the original movie Tarzan, held many a world swimming record. For years those records were unthreatened, no one could imagine being as good as Tarzan. Today 13- and 14-year-old boys and girls are swimming faster than old Tarzan.

Can you (ordinary you) do better? Can you do more? Can you do a thousand things at once? Have a 48-hour day? You sure can. Others do it, the producers you admire do it, and most of them are not as talented, well educated, or as young as you are. Then what's wrong with you? Probably nothing, maybe you've just never seriously considered doing more, maybe never realized the rewards for it. We can get in a rut or set way or system of doing things, doing the same thing the same way for the same pay, and never realize anything is wrong... until a competitor—another person or country—drastically outperforms us and takes our position, our spirit, and maybe even our spouse away from us.

ACCOMPLISHMENT, THE GREAT MOTIVATOR

It's accomplishment that really motivates. Dreams, promises, stories, and projections of success are nothing compared to a taste of success! Getting ready to do can generate some enthusiasm, but nothing turns us on like "finished." "I did it." "Done!" "Mission accomplished." Once you've moved a mountain, or even a molehill or two, you'll find yourself clicking your heels and ready to start on the next.

For a doer, one accomplishment just provides the fuel for more! Stokes the fire, makes it burn brighter!

Yes, you can do more, and once you get started, you'll never want to stop.

WHAT'S THE CATCH?

It seems that whenever we have a real conviction and determination to upgrade or change ourselves, some big shadow of suspicion slows us down or backs us off. Right now I can hear you cautiously asking, "What am I going to have to **DO** (buy, learn) **for my 48-hour watch?** Relax—nothing hard, strange, or expensive, in fact to do more you start by doing less. The "shed" chapter is next.

PRODUCTIVITY TEST OF TRAITS

Check the boxes—which are you?
Then add up the checkmarks and score yourself in each column.

LOW PRODUCER
- ☐ Generally late
- ☐ Looks for less to do
- ☐ Lays low when wounded
- ☐ Avoids hard work
- ☐ Plays a lot
- ☐ Watches the clock
- ☐ Lives in the past
- ☐ Often out of control
- ☐ Sleeps excessively
- ☐ Maximum amount of TV
- ☐ Passive
- ☐ Makes excuses
- ☐ Lives by tradition
- ☐ Must be asked
- ☐ Easily distracted
- ☐ Follower
- ☐ Whines about injustices
- ☐ Waits
- ☐ Plays it safe
- ☐ Walks

☐ **TOTAL**

Scoring
18-20 You may be beyond help!
13-17 Read this book twice and put it into practice!
11-16 Not quite good enough! Read the rest of the book and you'll be sure to do better.
9-15 Average... that doesn't really cut it in the world of high producers.
4-9 Be proud of yourself! (And keep it up!)
1-3 You're awesome! Nobody's that good!

HIGH PRODUCER
- ☐ Always early
- ☐ Looks for more to do
- ☐ Works while wounded
- ☐ Enjoys hard work
- ☐ Plays enough
- ☐ Races the clock
- ☐ Learns from the past
- ☐ In control of self
- ☐ Sleeps as needed
- ☐ Minimum amount of TV
- ☐ Active
- ☐ Makes it happen
- ☐ Sets new precedents
- ☐ Takes the initiative
- ☐ Hard to distract
- ☐ Thinker/leader
- ☐ Accepts injustices
- ☐ Goes ahead without if necessary
- ☐ Takes risks
- ☐ Runs

☐ **TOTAL**

Scoring
18-20 You're awesome! Nobody's that good!
13-17 Be proud of yourself! (And keep it up!)
11-16 Average... that doesn't really cut it in the world of high producers.
9-15 Not quite good enough! Read the rest of the book and you'll be sure to do better.
4-9 Read this book twice and put it into practice!
1-3 You may be beyond help!

A Little Subtraction...
Adds a Lot of
Production

One afternoon in the "old corral" back on the ranch, I was out in the middle of the herd doing my utmost to catch one of the steers to check its eye infection. Even with just one good eye, the steer was successfully eluding me. It would run around, through, and behind the fifty other cows in the corral (who thought I was after them, too). The other cows, with tails arched and hooves flying, were racing around everywhere. They would shield the infected steer, jump in front just as I was tossing the rope, get in my way when I was trying to run him down, etc., totally frustrating my efforts. My dad let me chase and toss until my throat was dry from manure dust, then said, "If you'd get some or all of those other cows out of there, you'd handle the one easier." I did, and caught my critter on the first toss.

How often do we find ourselves trying to focus on a task or goal, while scores (even hundreds) of other things are milling around it, leaping and crowding and hanging and bouncing in our way—creating confusion and eating up time. As in my case, these other "cows" are not necessarily bad nor do they need to be banished forever, but they sure need to be out of the way while you get on with the program at hand. Here is a case where **subtraction** will usually mean some real additions.

You are going to love this part of getting more time to use, because I'm not going to load you down with any thick planner notebook or elaborate filing system, recommend any programs, classes, or courses, teach you any theories, formulas, or clever maneuvers. I'm not going to ask you to drill yourself in anything, only to **discard**.

That means shed, toss, ditch, dump whatever is burying your 48-hour clock. You already have a 48-hour clock, you see, you already have "the time"—all the time you need—all you have to do is uncover it, find it, and use it.

I know you want some specifics now, so here is a list of some of the "stuff" suffocating your 48-hour clock. Some of these are actually good and worthwhile things; it's when they exist **in excess** that they become a problem.

DEJUNK!

The number one, the very first step to becoming a "more doer," a high producer, is to stop accumulating and start eliminating. In other words, **dejunk!**

You just can't cruise in a crowd. So dump the time robbers. I'm referring not only to that junk in your attics, garages, and closets, and all the other useless things we spend so much time buying, storing, shuffling, and sorting, but less tangible things like habits and associates that waste time.

It doesn't take any advanced degrees to figure out that it takes time to tend excess, the frills, the extras, all the physical and mental litter we carry around. It's so logical, yet so seldom done. We usually don't toss the trivia till we're forced to, or until we get serious about excelling, reaching our peak performance. I saw a college picture of one of my cleaning company managers, for example, with his head shaved. The reason was that he was a competitive swimmer, and not only hair but even a button or emblem on a swimsuit slowed you down. Howard Hughes totally redid a superb airplane two days

after it was finished because he found a flatter, non-wind-catching rivet.

Trimming the trivia and trashing it is fun, it costs nothing, and has guaranteed results—more available time.

Get Rid of Those Excess Objects

At even the very busiest times in my life, I've found I could almost double my output by dejunking.

Junk and clutter in and around our homes, lives, and workstations account for an amazing amount of wasted time and emotion. More arguments, family fights, divorces, and business failures are the result of junk than of anything else except finances. Have you stopped to add up the amount of **life and time** we consume over ownership of things, possessions? Dejunk!

Keeping things neat and uncluttered is one of the best ways to ensure speed and efficiency. We can't do much go-getting if we have to constantly dig and hunt for what we need, and dodge and squeeze around things. Keeping no-account stuff around, or things that are no longer needed, is like keeping the scaffolding up after the building is built or painted. It looks bad and just gets in the way.

If you've done the job, you don't need to leave scraps and trimmings and leftovers around to prove that you did it, or how—the fact that the new structure stands is evidence enough. And if there's a lot of even high-class junk around, we spend a lot of time fiddling with it, polishing and protecting it. And the more we have, the more we accumulate. For what?

Get rid of anything you don't use or want. Don't love what can't love you back. Top producers are seldom junkers.

Prune Before You Prioritize!

There's a lot going on these days, even a sedate life of the 1990s is about three times as active as a barnstorming life of the 1920s. We're not just bombarded, we're saturated with information, events, offers, and opportunities. If we just go stand somewhere we can have more happen to us in ten minutes than in ten days of earlier times.

Sorting and processing all the new possibilities and problems dumped on us daily can, will, and does consume a lot of time. This isn't productivity, it's just activity. You can easily end up old, tired, and troubled, without having been anywhere or accomplished anything. How many times have you heard or said to yourself, "I've been running all day, I'm dead tired, and I haven't really gotten anywhere"?

In an effort to deal with all this, most people attempt to follow the great production principle called "prioritizing." This will get you nowhere except further buried and stressed out. So first, before you do anything else, ignore or weed out the unnecessary (you know what it is) and you won't have to labor over most of those great management words like delegate and prioritize.

Don't sit there trying to prioritize 10,000 "things to do"—it just uses up time like crazy and confuses you. Putting things in priority order isn't one hundredth as important as selecting the actually necessary out of the incredible number of things available to us each day. The first move of a real getter-doner is to **get rid of activities and options we don't really want or need, that are just muddying the water.** It's a lot easier to prioritize 1,200 things a year than 10,000, and a lot more of them are likely to actually get done. Don't put all those unnecessary things on your list and in your life just because they are there.

Eliminate that Excess Baggage

As I said earlier, even good stuff can bog you down if you have too much of it.

Carrying too much with you everywhere, for example, too much gear and too many helpers, ends up hurting the goal rather than helping. It's easy, with all good intentions, to spend so much time gathering equipment and help that we never get to the job. All of the people (the "army") and parts (the "ammunition") you might need for a task do have to be roomed and boarded, transported and tended.

Over the years, I've found that the more I've condensed my tools, vehicles, library, wardrobe, travel kit, and suitcase contents, the more I get done. Before, with a 24-hour clock, when I moved from task to task I had to have a pickup to haul all my stuff in. As I gradually reduced the size of my arsenal and eliminated duplication in my equipment, shook things down to the essentials, I found I could still manage to do the job—and now I didn't have to manage a bunch of things. I used to carry a big axe and a little hatchet in my tool box, now I have one middle-sized axe, which means one thing less to lose and look for, or blame someone else for carrying off after I've left it lying around.

NOISES AND DISTRACTIONS

Observing a noticeably unproductive student/part time clerk attempting to fill inventory in my cleaning supplies store, I asked him about the radio blasting beside him and the TV in the background (he was trying to catch the news while he was at it, too). "How can you pay attention to what you're doing?" I said.

"I need the noise to concentrate," he said.

Lights buzzing, machines whirring, music or TVs blaring, nonstop traffic noise, clearly audible nearby conversations... people may say they can tune things like this out (and maybe some can). But one way or another distractions feed into your system, and chip away at and compete with your concentration.

The mind has to absorb and process **all** input, and background noise backs down your production level. Some kinds of soft music or white noise have been claimed to speed up output a little, but plain old observation of results will tell you that good producers do not need lots of noise.

Even if you're disciplined and on the job, distractions of any kind always take their toll. They blot out a lot of inspiration and use up energy. I used to be fond of saying that something might distract me, but it would never divert me. But now I know that continued distraction is bound to end up diversion. Like a pesky fly—first it's only a little distracting, then more and more, and finally the urge to end the buzzing and the challenge of killing the filthy thing totally occupies you.

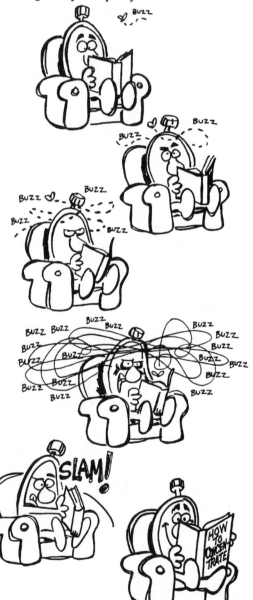

High producers know and stay away from their distraction weaknesses. Noise and distractions drown out too much of "your time."

INTERRUPTIONS

Control them when you have to accomplish something! Easier said than done, right? We do have some crowded days and weeks and times where eliminating interruption is not just impractical but close to impossible. However, folks, that's **not all the time.**

Amazing how things take care of themselves when we aren't there every minute, isn't it? Equally amazing, once we're away from the clamor and chaos, how much we get done. The older and wiser I get, the less time I spend in that assemblage of interruptions known as "**the office.**" I've seen times I got on the job or to the office first thing in the morning and did nothing but shuffle things, tee-hee, say hello to visitors, paw through junk mail, and chitchat for the first couple of hours—I was never able to start or finish anything. I finally had to get in the car and drive over to the park a couple of blocks away to do my day's work—uninterrupted—**in one hour!**

Interruptions sidetrack progress and alter our mood. And telephones, as you know, have no mercy. With constant interruption, a half-day's work can easily take three days.

When we're interrupted, we have to reorganize and start, reorganize and start, reorganize and start. A lot harder than organizing once and **doing.**

24

How Much Time Are You Losing to Interruption?

Beginning a project only to have to stop to get a tool or part, then repeat this a number of times, for example, really uses up time. You can easily spend a whole day taking care of interruptions, rather than working.

If you're not convinced yet, try this little exercise.

1. When you arise in the morning, list the things you intend to do that day as 1, 2, 3, 4, etc., at the top of a piece of paper.

2. Make another list called Interruptions (1, 2, 3, 4, etc.) in the bottom half of the sheet, leaving blank spaces after the numbers.

3. Get to work now immediately, and note the time you spend on each project, down to the minute.

4. Each time you're interrupted, mark the reason and how much time it took in the appropriate space.

Follow these instructions all day for two or three days. If you need any further convincing, at the end of this trial period figure up the total time lost to interruptions. Then compute how many of your planned accomplishments you could have completed in that time.

Control Your Visitors!

Keep yourself crowded with work, but not with people.

A great doer summed up her advice for a lifetime of success: "You can't be entirely social and get a lot done." We live to interact with and love people, but too many, too often, leaves us unable to accomplish much.

Visitors are fun and socializing is fun, even one of the leading ingredients in living a satisfying life. But if you aren't able to shut down the switch on this when you need to, it will consume your entire 24-hour day before you ever have a chance to make it 48.

The bottom line is that you cannot accept **all** invitations, attend **all** gatherings, take in **all** events, or stop to talk or chat whenever anyone and everyone wants to. Not because any of this is bad or worthless necessarily, but because so much of it just isn't important in your life right now, or in the direct line of what you need to do. It will also lead you off into other directions.

Remember, you are the **master of your own time**, not a helpless victim. You are the only one who can control your interrupters. "I wish they'd leave me alone" is a weak, spineless plea. You have to take things into your hands, and here are seven things you can do:

1. Make your operation patterns—your free and busy times—known to everyone. And train them to visit during the free, not the busy periods.

2. Let out the word that you "hate interruptions." (This works wonders, and by itself may eliminate at least 50% of the problem.)

3. Demand the courtesy of appointments, or at least advance warning. This makes it easier to stay productive and on track.

4. Be busy. When someone comes unexpectedly, always act busy or in the middle of something. Then you can either offer to stop or keep at it. Ninety-five percent will take the hint. The remaining five percent are too oblivious to take offense anyway.

This helps people get the message, and

if they assume that you're "always busy" they'll only make ten-minute calls, not the usual two hours. Being honestly busy limits, if not eliminates, unimportant interruptions. People seldom invade areas under heavy fire.

5. Redecorate to discourage dawdling. Sofas in an office, for example (besides taking up a lot of space that could be used productively), invite people to visit and stay. I only have one chair in my office… **mine**.

6. Become the aggressor, the initiator to end an interruption. Develop some stock phrases that suit you and use them. Learn to say things like "Well, thank you for coming" as a hint that you're moving on to something else. If that doesn't work, don't hem and haw or beat around the bush. Come right out with it. Say "Golly, it's too bad you happened to come right when I was in the middle of this project."

A magic sentence: "Gee, I'm sorry. Could we talk/get together another time?" Then *you* can arrange the stacking of bricks to get more done.

7. If all else fails, put them to use. Solicit their help and hand them a hard hat or pair of gloves or a dish towel or whatever.

Find whatever works for you, but do it. Welcome people that are scheduled, but for those that pop in and interrupt, give an abbreviated welcome and excuse yourself and get your work done, "Excuse me, but I have to have this package off to Fed Ex before noon, I sure hope you're enjoying your visit to this part of the world."

RUN-ON REPORTING

It is good, and sometimes important, to keep track of things, but this can go too far.

You can get so caught up in charting and chronicling the course that you never reach the destination. You can find yourself focusing on and rewarding reports instead of results. Or picking up and counting empty shells, instead of bringing home any game.

When we get too busy telling what we can do, we often don't have the time and energy left to do it. Some people get so enthusiastic about tracking and reporting and categorizing events they forget that **the event,** not the report, is the subject.

Necessary as they are, records are passive, a history of production or prediction of it—not production itself! Keeping track is good support for any tracks made, but it's making those tracks that is the target, not measuring and calculating the score.

FINANCE FIGHTING

Constant worry about finances—balancing, floating, borrowing, and all the other little activities involved in juggling and angling money is ultra time and energy consuming (if not all-consuming). Life is hard when you're forever fighting finances.

Early in my career, when expanding my business and having to meet large payrolls, I was spending three hours every day just begging for collectibles, hunting up, transferring, and taking care of money. About fifty percent of my waking thoughts and dreams were about it, too. If I had been using all that time for more constructive and progressive activities, I'd own three banks by now. **Stretching is great for physical fitness, and about the worst thing going for financial fitness**. Have you ever added up the time and money spent trying to scrounge up money?

Most of us assume we are cash short in business or our personal lives for reasons beyond our control, but few financial circumstances are beyond our control. Who can you actually blame it on? Generally it comes back to us, our excesses and our lack of discipline. The day I decided to quit spending cash I didn't have, quit cussing the bankers and collectors for my problems and start operating money ahead instead of money behind (on credit), I gained more time than I could believe.

We all can do this if we ease off and up a little. Force yourself to keep a cash reserve, quit spending to the end and hoping for a windfall. Keep your hands off the working money. Fighting finance, at home or in business, talking and arguing about it, covering bases, getting by the skin of your teeth, explaining and accounting for things, etc., is more draining than double the amount of physical toil. I'll wager this is one of your biggest nonproductive pastimes right now. It can be changed quite simply and when you quit the cash hassle your personal productivity will increase tremendously!

CORRECTABLE HEALTH PROBLEMS

None of us are completely innocent of this one, chewing on one side of our mouth or dodging certain foodstuffs because we won't go to the dentist, or limping around and spending several days down or "out" because it's inconvenient or costly to have that foot fixed. Or because we just want to keep on putting it off.

The consequences of genuine health needs are inevitable and delay will only accelerate the cost and pain. It also keeps you unfocused, concentrating on the pain you're enduring or the pull to come. All of which takes up or dilutes a major portion of "your time."

OVERDONE SOCIAL EVENTS

There's a party going on all the time somewhere... and for hours. People get together and "kill" time (like every evening after work). A lifetime can easily go by that way. Fun is fun and getting together can be a real highlight of living and loving, but **focusing on partying isn't going to get you far**. Life isn't a party, and real doers don't have the time to waste. Showing up and standing around at every social event in the world isn't going to do a thing for accomplishment, it will only fog your watch crystal.

At every convention or trade show I'm hired to speak or perform at, for instance, there is always a cocktail party. People hang on each other's arms in a cloud of cigarette smoke, gripping an iced glass of something as if their lives depended on it. Conversations are full of loud laughter, back patting, and snide remarks. People seem at their worst at a cocktail party, and parties and social events put us all in an easy non-focused frame of mind. And so most of the "I'll calls" and "please sends" and "how are things goings" end up forgotten or a waste of time as far as getting the job done. Even as a place to meet people, situations like this are rather diluted for proper bonding and even if they're well

dressed, people are seldom at their best at late hours, eating and drinking.

People will tell you that parties are necessary for getting acquainted and being promoted, that's bull. I show up on the real scene fresh and prepared the next morning, and guess who they all remember the best and even envy?

I'm sure the world changers belong to very few social clubs.

FOOD-CENTERED LIVING RITUALS

My mother-in-law was religious about scheduling things, especially meals. When it's time to eat, **everything** stops to eat, no buts about it. One afternoon a high wind came up and blew some trash out of my burning barrel and caught the hillside near our house on fire. The fire only had to burn about 200 feet across our yard to reach the brush, and once it did that, it would burn up everything from our ranch to the city, about 20 miles of dry brush away.

It was a desperate situation, and I was alone. I grabbed buckets and shovels and rags and went to work on the flames and

was killing myself just keeping even. The smoke and heat from both the fire and the 100-degree weather was so bad I could scarcely breathe or swallow, the hair on my arms and my eyebrows was singed, and my pant legs kept catching fire, but I couldn't stop. When I was right on the verge of getting slightly ahead of the fire line, saving 80,000 acres of pasture grass and trees and a city, my mother-in-law strolled up to the edge of the fire and hollered in a shrill voice, "It's time to eat—now—come right now, you've got to learn to take care of yourself!" The whole countryside was about to go up in smoke and she wanted to interrupt me for something as incidental as eating!

If eating is the central focus in your life, the thing you plan everything around and you intend to keep it that way, don't count on becoming a great getter-doner. One of my contracting companies, for example, once had 112 painters literally standing around waiting for the scaffolding to arrive for a big painting job. When it finally was delivered (by one of my managers) he was forty-five minutes late. His excuse: "Well, I hadn't had lunch, so I stopped down the road to eat."

He didn't have a clue that **a skipped, later, or quick meal once in a while means a day or a weekend (or over a lifetime, five or six years, at least) gained to get things done,** and to nourish the soul and other people.

When you find yourself burning so hard, accomplishing so much that you have to ask, "Did I eat today?" you are getting nearer to the refined fire of self-discipline. Eating well and regularly doesn't have to mean centering life on food, as so many people do. Don't let eating ceremonies such as stopping to eat a big formal meal stand in the way of accomplishment.

No, I'm not getting ridiculous, but making (on an ordinary workday) eating into an elaborate ritual instead of a refueling process is nonproductive. Some people spend three to four hours per day just *eating*. You can still enjoy your food and family associations at meals if you cut that down to one hour a day.

When I first started to do a lot of traveling, doing media shows and seminars, speaking, etc., my productivity seemed to fall. I didn't seem to be getting as much done as I once did.

Why? Every town I showed up in, twenty people with the publisher, the network, the station, or other sponsor were determined to dine their special guest on the expense account, and they'd all planned and picked the nicest and most ceremonial eating place in town to take me. And as a courtesy, and sometimes because I was hungry, I would go. So each night in a different town meant new people and new places, great food, great company.

Some of those meals, however, were taking three hours or even more from the time we left the hotel until we returned. Little business was accomplished, it was noisy, the food was overpriced and overspiced, and on every side were waiters with phony accents, playing up to you for tips. I suddenly realized I was losing up to thirty hours a week in the new travel world just eating!

Now even if I'm by myself in the middle of nowhere, I seldom eat out and I get a lot more done. I'm in better health, and it doesn't really offend anyone not to spend $30 or $40 of their money for a meal! I don't have to be irritated by overdone "amenities" anymore, or smokers and noises, lines and crowds. And I give my tip money to charity now and have my thirty hours of time back.

SHOPPING

Shopping is one of the most nonproductive pastimes around. Buying what you need, when you need it, is a necessary and important part of life, but "shopping" isn't. The majority of people who go shopping (wandering aimlessly through the shops and malls, taking in all the latest offerings), are low producers, strangers to a 48-hour day. Shopping is extending buying into a social event, which uses up tons of time, and ultimately weakens and confuses you

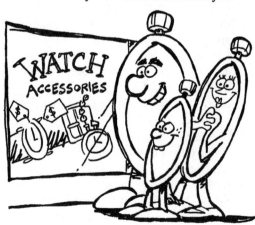

into buying things you didn't really want or need or can't afford. High producers buy, but seldom shop. But they miss bargains, you say? **A quick and nontiring overpaying for something may beat a drawn out and labor-intensive underpaying for it**. Think about it. You'll seldom see high achievers, super doers, big movers... shopping.

IMAGE PURSUITS

Trying to be seen as the Duke and Duchess of your subdivision is a real timetaker. Getting hung up on the image and status of our home and car, trying to conduct ourselves so as to elevate ourselves socially is a waste of time. Who really cares? Those who don't have what you have will just hate you for having more and showing off (and you won't even get respect because they'll assume you cheated somebody out of or embezzled it). Those on the same level with you won't like you either, for trying to be as good as them, and those above you, like the neighbor with two Mercedes and an albino poodle, will consider you unnecessarily pretentious.

Having a bunch of glitzy belongings gets you nowhere. It just enriches the junk merchants and the insurance companies. And the big uno—all this takes **time** and resources to tend.

BEST DRESSED STRESS

Wonder how many years of our life clothes take? In all the time and motion studies and analyses we see, I've never heard anyone ever say a word about dress and dressing. All that time spent picking out clothes, putting them on, changing and adjusting them—all that strutting in front of others and the mirror.

Fast movers want quick clothes, too. The other morning, for instance, my wife offered to pack my shirts and asked me which ones I wanted. "The productive ones," I answered. She came out of the closet with a perplexed look: "Just what is a productive shirt, may I ask?"

"The ones without the two buttons on each sleeve and the button-down collar." It takes three times as long to put on and do up a shirt like this. I'm not into clip-on ties for speed yet (I've been tying ties for so long I can do it in seconds), but in general the less laces and buttons and belting and snapping and matching and tucking to do before getting going, the better I like it. Somehow I've also managed to survive well without wearing jewelry of any kind. Not because I don't like it, but just because it uses up more time putting it on and taking it off, not to mention guarding it, and looking for it after you set it down somewhere or drop it down the drain.

Fancy or overly daring clothes can cut productivity on the job, too. We can't run, bend, climb, or even breathe deeply (because our outfit won't permit it), or we're so preoccupied with how good we look that what we're supposed to be doing is lost in the shuffle.

"Dressing for the express lane" might sound a little radical, but it sure speeds up a lot of speedy people I know. As a rule the heavy dressers and high stylists are the slowest people on two legs and the biggest time consumers.

The same is true for the other grooming and gussying preoccupations, from hair care to makeup. You'll never be effective if vanity overrules sanity.

In the office, the classroom, or at home, production is cheaper and more effective than sagless silicone transplants, $50 an ounce perfume, hairpieces, and all of that. People love deeds and ignore duds!

RUBBISH READING

I know reading is automatically considered worthwhile, if not sacred, and there's no shortage of reading material today. There are more than 50,000 new books published every year, tens of thousands of magazines around of every imaginable type, and daily and weekly newspapers all over the place. Reading takes time, lots of it. If the material is **good and beneficial** then it's a productive, enjoyable pastime; if not, you're squandering time and brain cells.

I'm a writer myself, but I'll be the first to tell you that much of what's written and peddled in the form of the printed word is not too profound. Magazines for example (except for the more technical ones) are neutral, middle of the road material. They aren't going to come forth with anything that takes a hard stand and changes your behavior and buying habits, if it might offend any of their sponsors. If I wrote an article about the vacuum cleaner banditry going on today (where you pay $600 for a unit worth about $99) and if it were a true, helpful, moneysaving article, do you think your favorite home magazine would publish it? Never! It would cost them hundreds of thousands of dollars an issue in lost advertising. Likewise, books that couldn't matter less to your life or any-

one else's fill the shelves of bookstores and airport and drugstore book racks.

Relieve yourself of that rubbish reading, and there'll be more time for those things you really want to do.

"WORKED UP FOR NOTHING" STUFF

Why Elizabeth Taylor is suffering from acute insecurity, or why some soap opera star just got kicked out of someone's bed, can really erode your might and mind (as well as your agenda) if you take the time to track it... and for what?

This really came home to me one day after watching "my team" lose a big game on TV. I really get into a game and take everything personal, and when I turned off the set, I was irritated and exhausted for hours afterward. I'd seen this happen several times now, and I realized I had to quit watching if I planned to do anything productive afterward. Don't let your adrenaline be drained by things that aren't even real, and **not rewarding**.

We waste millions of hours a minute around the world on things like this. The latest big storm is about to hit the eastern seaboard, for example. It's going to be the biggest yet and everyone is told to prepare for it. News is in short supply at the time, so the network begins a campaign of speculating about it. **What will happen if**? And they build on this until they have four days of tension and nonexistent-as-yet problems solved. Four days of nothing but talk and theorizing. Then the storm backs off and nothing happens. Things like this take your time and emotion and give you nothing back.

Remember the time the U.S. accused a Russian ship in a Nicaraguan harbor of having a MiG jet aboard? There wasn't much news available right then either, so the media, in their usual trivial pursuit, expanded this question—Is there such a plane on the ship or not?—into full-time fare on the talk and interview shows. There was no real evidence the planes were there, no one saw any, our spy plane saw little boxes not big enough for a lawn mower, the Russians denied having any planes on board, but we called experts in and interrogated them and asked clever questions like, "George, on a scale of one to ten what are the chances of a MiG being in those little boxes?" George, who was from Sagebrush City and had barely read the news reports, grumbled wisely and gave it a four.

Worrying about things we have no control over, or that are really none of our business, can use up a lot of time. You can easily spend two full hours a day just digesting, talking and thinking about, and using up emotion on things that have absolutely no worth at all to you or anyone else. That in fact are downright detrimental.

On my way to a speaking engagement one morning, I jotted down a sample of the daily menu of trivia available to us. One paper (people were laboring through all 78 pages of it that Sunday) had an exact count and description of the number of pairs of shoes Mrs. Marcos of the Philippines owned, a whole page forecasting and predicting the weather for the week ahead, and detailing the weather of the week past (neither of which we can do anything about), articles glorifying the life of losers in detail, tons of descriptions and praises of new stuff we don't need, a literary critic analyzing which side of the raft Huck Finn got in, accounts of the expression in a convicted criminal's eyes when the electric chair was activated, a summary of urine reports on 72 Olympic athletes, how one might get a peek at Cher's tattooed buttocks, the latest Israeli/Arab argument (a story now 5,500 years old), the latest big politician's womanizing adventures, disposing of leftover Desert Storm t-shirts, etc.

This kind of sawdust can lead your life, or **YOU** can, and the decision you make here will have a lot to do with whether you become a high producer or not. Even a great man or woman could get lost in this sea of stuff that matters zero in your life. And will add up to zero in the future, too. You can't spend your time and emotion tending trivia day after day.

You alone can make the value judgment here—you know what's really contributing to your life and goals and what isn't. If you can't do anything about it, or it doesn't affect the outcome of your life or that of others you care about, then don't waste time arguing or worrying about it, or betting on it. You'll save a lot of hours by dejunking this stuff and have time to **make news** instead of reading it.

TEARS OVER SPILT MILK

I broke a window once and was pretty despondent over it—"Don't cry over spilt milk," my mother said. At the age of eight, I couldn't see much of a relationship between milk and windows, but I sure do now.

One of the poorest ways to use time, in fact the most useless, is "stew time."

When something is over and done with and yields some unalterable result, stewing, moping, fuming, and fretting over that outcome is a totally rewardless consumption of the hours and minutes of our lives. Working up a lather when there's nothing there to wash is futile, yet most people will keep their hot plate on simmer or even boil for a day (or even months and years) after all is over with. This particular form of self-punishment is a popular pastime, even though no one even admires you for all your suffering, how well and passionately you apply yourself to spending time so stupidly.

Agitation and production are not even in the same vocabulary. Staying in a tizzy over a totally unchangeable thing just throws your production gear into neutral so you burn up all your fuel sitting still.

As a contractor who often worked for and genuinely admired the world's best telephone operation, I bawled and argued over the breakup of the Bell System for months, until I finally decided "Hey, it isn't right but I'm not going to change it. It's going to mean poorer service and higher phone costs for all of us, **but it's done** and I'm not going to be able to do a thing about it. So I better forget it and earn more to pay the bills."

Don't spend your time and effort dwelling on events or circumstances that can't be stopped, restored, redirected, or resolved. (You know exactly what things I'm talking about.) Anguishing over past losses—people or profits—is a 100% nonproductive activity. Don't dwell on or mire yourself in emotional turmoil over old injuries or things you can't do anything about. Spilt milk laps up lots of time.

THE NAWERS

Nawer? That means something that's gnawing or nagging at you, generally not a little face-it-in-a-moment thing, that's bugging and worrying you constantly, causing stress and anxiety you really don't need right now.

On the ranch we called it a burr under the saddle or a pebble in the boot, meaning you can still ride and still walk, but do so with restricted motion. Aiming for a 48-hour day does not allow much restricted motion! The short stop it takes to unsaddle or remove your boot and dislodge the irritant is always worth the interruption.

If you can feel any nawers gnawing then you better denaw. It's like having something in your eye. If it's in there good you

SPILLED MILK

WASTED TEARS

either have to get it out or it will put you out, even the tiniest grain of metal or sand. I've tried rubbing and blinking and ignoring little problems like this and none of it works. If you leave them there they do damage. There are enough unpreventable ruinations around without setting yourself up for anything more.

Guilt and Grudges

Are among the worst of the nawers.

A clear conscience is a big key to production. Confucius, who may not have known he was speaking about personal productivity, said, "There are three marks of a superior man, being virtuous, he is free from anxiety, being wise, he is free from perplexity, being brave, he is free from fear." Every one of those three virtues frees up time.

When you analyze what really consumes time and energy, nothing rates higher than **anxiety.** When you do an evil deed, you have the constant anxiety afterward of worrying about getting caught and are constantly using up good logic and energy and creating rationalizations, just in case you are found out. So if you have done something that's keeping you up nights, apologize, confess, pay up, or whatever, but don't

keep carrying it around with you. It's eating away at your time.

Bearing grudges and nursing hard feelings is a real time and spirit waster, too— it takes lots of effort to keep score. Playing and replaying, in our mind and to others, the injustices we've endured, what someone said and did and what we said or did then, etc., etc., is fruitless all around. Uncomplicate things—forget it. If something is bugging you, some hard feelings or a little vendetta in the family or at work, either drop it and get it out of your mind, or go to the person and have it out and get it over with.

Likewise, if you're carrying a burden of guilt or backlog of things you failed to do or take care of in the past, either forget them, or do whatever you have to do to make them right **right now.**

You'll get a lot more done and have a lot more fun… if you're unencumbered!

A duty dodged is like a debt unpaid; it is only deferred, and we must come back and settle the account at last.
—*J. F. Newton*

Pettiness

There lives not a person on this earth who doesn't pack the capacity for anger, jealousy, revenge, irritation, malice, and at least forty other unfortunate forms of related behavior. But the people who yield to these are seldom producers because they use the clock to count injustices. They spend most of their energy focusing on and overreacting to the everyday human failings of others, instead of helping us all to step beyond them to more important matters.

We call this pettiness, this constant bringing up and brooding over little tiffs and jealousies over position, promotion, someone's new car or escort. Soon a minor misstep or oversight is a major melodrama. I've seen people lose three hours of work over losing their place in the cafeteria line or the luggage claim, as they ranted and had to describe this invasion of their line space by some inconsiderate and obnoxious interloper to everyone. That's petty, and it only gets in the way of production. Pettiness charges for its time, too—time and a half!

THE BIG FIVE MOST WANTED TIME BANDITS

1. Beverage Rituals

I vote for "beverage rituals" as the most deadly opponent of the 48-hour day. If we don't lick this, the Lord is going to have to go back to the drawing board and make one of our arms crooked, with a cupped hand. It seems everyone is forever clutching a mug of coffee or "Giant Gulp" of pop—at their desk, in the car, or anywhere. What a nuisance to have to keep track of, as well as addictive, unhealthy, unsightly, expensive, and a stain and cleanup problem. But worst of all is the amount of time **tending** such things takes out of our life—it's incredible.

The average American drinks 56,000 cups of coffee in a lifetime, for example. Even if you don't brew it yourself, that's 56,000 times you have to find your cup, fill it, add cream or sugar, carry it to your

work station, pick it up, set it down (repeat this at least 14 or 15 times), then dump the part that got cold.

With modern air-conditioned and plush offices and short workdays, 30 minutes or more a day spent on "coffee breaks" does nothing to increase productivity. What it does accomplish is to spread and encourage gossip and contempt and criticism of the employer, customers, etc. Then too, of course, breaks have to be increased and extended.

Look around at your next coffee break, few if any of the high producers will be there (and that ought to tell you something).

You can use your time to sip, or to zip through the assignments of life.

---

2. Over-Sleeping

There's no lack of sleep analyzers, and when magazines get hard up for an article someone is always happy to expound on the art of sleeping, or a new theory of sleep needs. There are always revolutionaries who say four hours is enough for anyone, and those who insist eight hours or more plus maybe a nap at noon is the only way to go through life.

Most people have a clear concept of the amount of sleep they need, and it's purely a personal preference. If you want to be more productive, reducing your sleeping to just enough time to get a good rest is the answer. The best producers I know are get-up-early-in-the-morning people. I hardly ever see a late or oversleeper accomplish much. Try cutting even an hour off your sleeping, and keep yourself stimulated so you won't need a nap because you're bored, and watch how much more work you get done.

Early to bed, early to rise, your available time grows in size.

---

3. Lounging

Rest is a productive pastime, but lounging isn't. Millions survive worldwide without one single hour of lounge time at home, on the beach or in the tub, etc. Rest is spending time restoratively (it could be working, playing, sleeping, thinking, etc.). Lounging is unhooking, being idle, adrift in time and from the situation at hand—loitering, bumming, dawdling, and droning around is what mind and body do when you lounge. This is all generally nonproductive. Resting just holds up the goings-on while you take a breather; lounging checks you out of them and they go on or away without you! Avoiding lounge-related places or practices will only advance your 48-hour watch.

4. Play Time

Psychologists have drilled into us the idea that we need tons of play to offset our

work or we're out of balance. Everyone is convinced they need a release (mostly from jobs they're doing little on). So we buy boats, scooters, snowmobiles, and other gismos which cost a lot and make us feel guilty if we don't use them. Recreation *is* productive and great for a change, as are vacations. But our kids are raised learning more about time-off activities than how to achieve or produce.

Don't get too concerned about the percentage of play time in your life. The most energetic, dynamic, enthusiastic, positive, and popular people I know play less than the average or hardly at all. Excess playing is nonproductive, it gives little back in later years and does nothing to build either lives or security. Constant pleasure seekers just get fat and lazy and drizzle their life away. Most high producers find their play in their work.

Relaxation needs a foundation to rest on—one called "industry," or "work," if you'd prefer a four-letter word. Well planned and chosen play can be therapeutic, educational, and productive...**if** it's counterbalanced with work.

You can do crossword puzzles to develop and enjoy the use of words, or you can write articles or books. You can pedal a stationary bike or go out and make a garden. When you're finished you have something besides exercise. Why not go for pastimes that have some net worth?

5. *Spectatoring*

Sure we all love to watch a ball game, movie, or boat race, but continually? We'd end up with nothing except time used up. These things are, after all, just games or performances, not real life. Like most of you, I love sports and events, but if we spend too much time watching others do all the moving and doing, we'll soon be eliminated from the game.

Spectatoring is one of the easier nonproductive pastimes to fall into. All we have to do is stop a few minutes, and the spectacle at hand takes over our mind and wits. Sometimes we need a break like this, but big-time watchers are seldom big producers!

The average American spends 2,600 hours a year being a spectator or listener. More than half of this time—1,460 hours a year—is spent on television. That means the average one of us is spending 4 hours a day (**12 years** of our entire life!) watching TV. Impressive, that one activity could occupy so much of our time. But it does and most TV time is totally nonproductive. Television offers the greatest variety of ways to waste time imaginable. A football game, an informational program, or a movie or two is great and a blessing to sit in our living room and experience, but four to five hours a day for weeks and months and years on end is not a blessing, more like immobilization and decay.

If you can't seem to get much done lately, switch off the TV, move it out, or drape a quilt over it for a month. You'll think you're a resurrected being! Your productivity will make such an upswing it'll leave you breathless, and you'll even feel better physically.

This list could go on for the rest of the book, but you know your own junk and clutter better than anyone. I just want to get you thinking of how easy some simple surrendering is, in exchange for access to a 48-hour day. Time to do all those "wants and wishes," all those things that've been waiting, that you've been holding back.

Notice I haven't said much about *how* to dejunk these things. I've called your attention to them, confident you already know how, and I promise that the time you gain will make it worth your while to act. If you need more guidance or convincing than this, there are two bestselling books called *Clutter's Last Stand* and *Not for Packrats Only*. Get them and read them—you'll enjoy them and they'll turn your life around.

Real producers have or get the guts to make the cuts when and where they're needed. "Lean and mean" they call it. But once you're lean, you don't generally have to be mean... 'cause you have all that extra time.

"But I just don't have the time..."

Say It No More

"I want to, I'd like to, I will... as soon as I have the time."

After doing TV appearances with and later reading the reports of some "time analyzers" (who actually studied how and where we use it all)—I bet we can find a few weeks or days or years to do that thing you really want to do. The average American, according to these experts, in his or her **lifetime** spends:

1,086 days "sick"

Three years in meetings

Eight months opening junk mail

Seventeen months drinking coffee and soft drinks

Two years on the telephone

Five years waiting in line

Nine months sitting in traffic

Four years cooking and eating

A year and a half grooming

A year and a half dressing

Seven years in bathrooms

Twelve years watching TV

Three years shopping

One year looking for misplaced items

24 years sleeping

Some of these things you could **cut by 50%** and only be better off for it. That will give you back at least ten years of precious time!

THAT SURPRISING SPARE TIME

If you could push a button and have a count of your "off" (wasted, lazy, occupied with nothing) hours for the last year, you'd discover that most of us have at least 1,500 hours of "spare time." What if those could be converted to productive accomplishments and handed to you as a surprise? Such as:

1. A check for $8000

2. Sixteen articles written for major magazines

3. A certificate indicating that you did indeed learn to play the piano

4. Forty thank-you letters from charities, hospital visits

5. Seven good books read

6. City-wide Top Yard and Garden award, 1996

7. Coach of the Year for helping three junior teams

8. Two paintings finished; Blue ribbon at the fair

9. Two college classes completed (six credit hours)

10. Refund check from health insurance, $821 (too busy to get sick).

All of this—or more—you could do with your off, idle, wasted hours. If all of this was yours, do you think you'd be dragging butt at the end of the year? Not a chance! You'd be leaping and strutting like a new colt in high clover!

One afternoon I ran into a friend who had struggled with a weight problem forever. He'd fought it and fought it and hated every minute of it. He'd been on diets and every milkshake meal ever invented, but to no avail. My friend was trim and happy now. "How?" I asked. "You know, Don, it was something so simple. I was told to make a list of all and what I ate. That sounded stupid, but I did it. Every time I ate something, I wrote it down... every little morsel. And man, what a surprise when I finished writing. I had a list twelve times as long as the one I kept in my mind. I found out I was eating enough for four people. It didn't seem like it when I was snacking and piecing. Once I saw the numbers, I was awakened to my problem. I'd sure underestimated what I ate!"

How much time we have and waste is surprising, too! Write yours down for a week—add up all the big and little pieces spent doing what—and you'll see not just pounds but tons of useless activities. A lot of them are things you don't even enjoy, so toss them off and out of your life.

One of my own average days, for example, might analyze out as follows:

Sleeping—6 hours

Grooming—15 minutes

Eating—45 minutes

Interview or other media activity—
2 hours

Speaking/Seminars—2 hours

Writing—4 hours

Meetings—30 minutes

Cleaning company business—1 hour

Church—15 minutes

House Cleaning/Home Maintenance—
1 hour

WHAT ABOUT THE OTHER 6 1/4 HOURS? The point exactly! I have 6+ hours to do more of what I want and like to do.

CHAPTER FOUR

The Mainspring: Direction

We've all tried it, to assemble or make something without a set of directions. The results are usually disgust, disaster, or downright ridiculous. Yet the task is clear, all the parts are there, and we've seen others like it and others do it. And we have all the tools, so why not figure it out as we go along?

I've laid down and bawled after attempting to build or fix something when the directions were not in the box (missing!). It usually triples the time involved and you almost always have to backtrack. When you have the directions you do it right, and it's much easier and faster.

Direction without an "s" is just as important. It's the dynamo of doing, the mainspring of your 48-hour clock. If you don't have it, all hands (yours and your watch's) will swing wildly.

I've seen talented, wholesome, eager young men flounder, fall, and fail, sure candidates for bumhood. Then they join the military and suddenly they emerge as a disciplined, organized person of character and confidence. The military is no shrink or Sunday school, but it does have one real strength and that's direction. It's saved a lot of potential drifters. I've seen athletic teams loaded with talent and desire thrash and fumble until a new coach stepped in and outlined a direction. Trace most teenage troublemakers' biggest lack, you'll find it's direction. Business failure, marriage failure—check it out and you'll find out there was no clear **route**, **rules**, or **reason** there when the package was opened. Try to make

anything human function without direction and you are doomed from the start.

Lots of direction comes quietly and naturally from good parents, teachers, and friends, but too many people "make it up as they go along" rather than make any kind of map to chart their course in life. I guess I've always taken direction for granted. One evening I was having an in-depth conversation with my wife and we were discussing how we might assist several friends who were depressed, stressing out, or unfulfilled. I told my wife I could see no reason why—these particular people were dripping with talent, education, and ability, in an excellent position to pick their work, location, or associates. "Yes," Barbara said, "but they haven't a clue as to what they want or where they are going."

Bingo, summary!

They had no direction. They had better sails than others, but they couldn't or wouldn't ever set the sail. They just stuck it up in the wind and had been blown all over the ocean of life all their lives. They may have had some thrills, but they didn't reach any ports. On the other hand, I've

POOR GUY... NEVER HAD A DIRECTION.

seen untalented, obnoxious, insensitive, lazy, even evil people do well, and live successful, happy, productive lives. All because they had a direction and stuck to it.

All kinds of great skills, instincts, and abilities come just with being born. Our senses are so marvelous, our built-in capacity to understand, love, and accomplish almost awesome. Every human has those, **but not necessarily direction.** Believe it or not, few people really know where they're going and why, even at the ages of 35-50. Life is going on all around them, and they just step out into it, hook up to someone, some cause, or some company, and wait to see where it takes them. They do sometimes choose a place to live, a job, or someone to marry. But at the bottom they don't know what they want or what they're after. They're just going to see what happens and react to it as it comes along. "I'll see what comes up" is their theme.

Motion alone doesn't mean much (except that you *are* alive)—it's **where** you're moving that matters. You may have heard the old joke, "I don't know where I'm going, but I'm making good time." Well, when you don't know where you're going or why, you **can't** make good time, plus you won't even know it when you get there!

We've all heard someone say, "Boy, that guy is lucky, he always seems to be in the right place at the right time." It isn't luck, it's direction. That "guy" has chosen a road to travel, a way and a time. Human imperfection might cause us to sometimes run off the road, pick the middle of the road, or run out of gas on our road, but once we've decided, chosen a direction, we have a road to follow.

What do I mean by direction here? Our own choices about the ethical standards and health rules we want to live by, the education and career we want to pursue, our responsibility to our society and country, our relationship with our family and other loved ones in the years ahead. You cannot waffle or wait on this. Notice how many people find themselves stopped at a serious intersection in life, before making these decisions. If you have direction, you know before the stop which turn to take.

Don't wait for a crossroads or a cross boss before attempting to figure out where you are going with your life and projects. Do it now! If you just drift along with what happens to be there or available right now, someone else's opinion, what Dad or Mom did, or the ACT test said you were cut out to be, you'll never be a top accomplisher. You won't be a producer, just a performer. Someday, better now than later, you have to settle on a direction—a cause, a purpose, an anchor, a guiding light. Do it, and it will keep you from wandering a crooked, forever searching path.

WHEN YOU HAVE FIRM DIRECTION IN YOUR LIFE:

• Your conflicts lessen and your energy increases. Direction is the best energizer in the world. It's pure magic for motivation, too. As a youth leader I've noticed that once kids have a clear direction and a cause, they'll double their output. My work crews on the job are the same. People who know what they're here for and why, what they want and what they're after, have by far, the most energy.

• It'll give you persistence. Staying with it, enduring to the end is essential for any accomplishment in life. It's hard to persist and endure when you don't know what for!

• Direction saves so much time. Once good health is our goal, for example, we don't have to ponder and anguish over menus and exercise opportunities, we know and can get on with it. Firm direction eliminates wavering and wondering.

• Direction will beckon and encourage outside help. People are happy to serve and assist people who know what they want and where they're going.

• Firm direction attracts good relationships. Direction radiates stability and we all cling to stable people and places.

• If you know where you're going, you'll know when you get there. You won't fail to recognize and savor the real accomplishments and rewards in your life.

WHAT ABOUT "CHARTS"?

Once you have your direction, your treasure map, do you post it, file it, or carry around with you? Where should this vital information be kept—in the head or heart, or on a clipboard in the hand?

The "charts" that are going to guide you to your destination in the wide world of doing are your own business, whether they should be big or little, computerized or memorized. I like to write mine down, to give them some reality, and I like to share them with others (see p. 51 and 81). And as for those goals themselves, my own personal rules for them are as follows:

YOUR Goals Should Be:

1. Your own—no one else can direct your life or set your goals.

2. Positive, not negative.

3. Ambitious enough to give yourself a good variety of projects to work on.

4. Attainable—it's okay to stretch yourself, but your goals must be reachable or you'll lose faith.

5. Exciting!—If what you're about isn't stimulating, I'd alter or change things

(yourself, your company, your setting, or your work menu) until it is!

6. Measurable—so you'll be able to tell where you are along the way.

7. Tied to a time frame—**when** you intend to accomplish them.

PICK THINGS THAT EXCITE YOU

After a seminar I gave to a large home extension group once, they were giving out awards, and I kid you not, word for word this came across the PA system:

"And now the next award is for the study of bubble size in beaten egg whites and its effect on the quality of angel food cake."

One woman at our table leaned over to another and said sarcastically, "Lord, is that ever exciting."

The excitement level of things does affect what we produce on them. When you keep things exciting, you keep them highly productive.

When we're excited about someone or something, we respond with energy and enthusiasm, brain and brawn. When we're stuck with an unexciting situation (companion or project), we may stick with it, but we don't do much with or about it. If we don't like what we're doing, aren't really for the cause or the undertaking, we'll ultimately only be about 25% effective.

Personal productivity really depends on zeroing in on the things that will bring excitement into your life, that's one big rule you have to follow. If you don't, you're going to spend your time carrying dead weight around, which is real dumb. When a group of self-made millionaires was ana-lyzed once to find what they might have in common, it turned out to be only one thing: they all enjoyed what they **did**, were doing what they liked to do. Their money basically came from following their hearts. The nice thing about that is if you follow your heart and make a million, great. If you don't, no problem, you still enjoyed the journey and that's the reason most of us are out to make a million in the first place, so we can enjoy ourselves.

No one can decide for you what is exciting.

Back on the ranch where I was raised, my dad never did like milking cows, though our neighbors all felt dairy cows were one of the few sure ways of getting paid regularly. Dad said they tied you down to the farm—twice a day, every single day, they had to be milked. We dreaded milking even a single cow, while our neighbors all looked forward to it!

Personally I couldn't be an accountant in Los Angeles if you paid me $1,000,000 a year for it, gave me a mansion and six months off a year. I happen to like outdoor, physical work and I could never live in a city. My whole life, direction, and schedule, from childhood on, has been attuned to this. But I know friends who wouldn't want their hands on a hoe handle. It's totally foreign to them, they don't like it, and are uncomfortable with it.

We're all basically the same, if we don't like something, we don't feel productive or happy doing it, so we don't do it. If you hate what you do, but stick to it because you have to (the security, prestige, etc.), you won't ever be a top producer, or reach your potential. Your 48-hour watch will have a dead battery. If you're simply putting in time, showing up until you can get another position (or waiting for weekends and vacation, relief) this isn't living, and it won't let you produce much either. It's kind of like asking someone to beat on you because it'll feel so good when they stop.

If you're in a situation like this, changing it is an important step to accomplish-

ment. So change the place, the assignment, the activity, the subject, your working partner, or whatever—as long as you're sure it's that thing—that's bogging you down.

If you're not sure whether it's you or the setting, here's a good question to ask yourself: "Are there things you will do, night or day, pay or no pay, simply because you like them?" Then you do have some productive drive in you. Reexamine your job choices and goals until you find something(s) you can feel that way about.

Notice we never have trouble getting started on the things we like to do? Does anyone have to tell us to start eating a pie a la mode? To say hi to that cute guy or gal, go to the beach, take a luxurious hot bath or shower? Never! Things we like, we start.

Oddly, many people these days seem to feel it's the job's or boss's responsibility to see to it that they are happy on their job—that's crazy. If you don't enjoy what you do, it's 100% your fault, either for staying around, or for not doing something about it, not changing anything. **You** ultimately control your destiny. Maybe not every event that ever happens to you, but at least your attitude and feeling about what you do, where you work, and who you work with.

If you look forward to it, you'll go forward on it, not watching the clock or counting the pay or the credit, but just for the sheer joy of doing.

FOCUS ON RESULTS, NOT EFFORTS

As I was visiting one day with someone who was struggling to "get ahead" in life, she explained her frustrations, especially how discouraged she was about not being able to get around to many of the things she knew needed to be done.

I asked her to make a list of all the things she had to do, and it went like this:

1. Make granddaughter a new dress.

2. Get teeth fixed.

3. Speak at the PTA national conference.

4. Put in the garden.

5. Paint the living room.

6. Tell husband I lost all our vacation money in Las Vegas while at the home show convention!

7. Return waffle iron I borrowed eight years ago (neighbor has forgotten).

8. Go to Seattle to pick up an unfavorite relative.

9. Write that book I've always intended to.

Now the list was logical and intelligent, but just the opposite of how I'd go about it. These are "have to" type thoughts and plans, which don't do a thing for motivation. They focus on **the work, the effort, the chores,** instead of the glory. Thinking this way it's easy to come up with negatives: there really isn't any time to, the machine may not work right, I don't know what size she is; wonder if they could get someone else, I have nothing to wear; it'll hurt, I'll feel awful; I'll just get it started and a frost will come along and kill everything;

I hear paint causes cancer; maybe I should just say I was pickpocketed or leave the country; now that their kids are grown they probably never make waffles; I wonder if I can get sick next week…; I can't spell very well, I'll wait till I get a word processor.

Here's the way I'd rewrite, and think of that list:

1. Pick a pattern, choose material for granddaughter's dress. ("Oooh, pretty dress, thanks. Oooh, it's so nice.")

2. Call the dentist for appointment. (Boy, will I look good when he's done, and I'll be able to eat spareribs again.)

3. Select a topic and start research to speak to my fellow parents, and teachers. ("Tell us more. Hurray, Bravo, you really helped me!")

4. Buy seed, get ground ready for garden. (Yummm, corn on the cob, fresh strawberries, tomatoes, lettuce, ummm watermelons.)

5. Find a paint color that will really set off that room, get a good trim brush. ("That room is such a pleasure to be in now. When did you have it done? YOU did it? Yourself?!")

6. Watch for a good mood, figure best time and way to tell husband we're broke. (I can't wait to get that off my chest!)

7. Whip up a batch of my best Belgians and berries and knock on their door: "I never like to return a dish empty…" (They'll forgive me anything!)

8. Go to get Aunt Glenda. (Look at the

map and figure out an interesting new route to the airport. Get an ice cream on the way. A nice relaxing drive by myself before company gets here!)

9. Get a pad and start jotting down notes for MY book. (The one I've dreamed about. Let's see, I can only spend three weeks in San Francisco signing autographs, one week in France.)

My first reaction to any project is **the satisfaction and pleasure of the end result.** I never think about how much work, money, time, or pain it'll take. I just look at what things will be like when I get done, how good I'll feel, how famous, rich, or loved I'll be. After I relish and bask in that for a while, quivering about the rewards, then I look at the list again. Okay, to have a prettier smile and better bite, I'll go see my dentist.

It's like mothers having babies, pioneers crossing the plains, entering a marathon, going to war, cooking, or cleaning—if you look at it too long or dwell on the immediate inconvenience, pain, or risk, you'll never get started. Or if you do, you'll be timidly and reluctantly committed. How many pioneers or immigrants would have left their cozy homes if they'd dwelt on the fact they were going to freeze, sweat, starve, suffer, and maybe bury children on the way? They focused and decided on having their own land, the fruits of that land, and freedom.

This is a secret most highly productive people use. They don't get lost in the paperwork and footwork, the details of getting there, but plan and prepare for the cause, the result, the REWARD.

HIGH PRODUCERS DON'T IGNORE THE RULES!

Oh boy, now comes the sticky fingers on the steering wheel of direction. Even direction is regulated by rules. There have to be rules for the road, boundary lines, start and stop signals, dos and don'ts, nos and yesses, nows and laters, times and seasons. Society, like nature, has to follow laws or it won't function. Selling rules to anyone is a long tough process, this basically a baby's and child's first learning in life, learning to operate by the rules. When we're older we think we have options and exemptions, we're disillusioned with those rules and not so sure they fit us. Sinatra made a hit song out of "I did it my way" and we've all wanted to skip or ignore rules that interfere with our path or method, intentions or schedule.

Someone once said, "Obedience is the first law of heaven." I say, "Following the rules—not making your own—is the first law of successful direction." Consider not only those great rules called the Ten Commandments but the carefully constructed Constitution of our country, companies who have a right to set their rules, doctors/scientists who tell you the best health and safety rules, and nature's rules, which

if not followed will beat you to a pulp sometimes. Rules exist to **enable things to work smoothly, to protect and enhance us,** help us attain our goals and follow our direction. If you doubt that, you only have to stand back and observe that the most calm and efficient people, the high producers, are those who follow the rules, and those who make their own are the strugglers and stress sufferers.

Sure you have the freedom to obey or follow the rules or not, but you don't have freedom from the consequences. And those consequences can foul up a life as well as a project or agenda.

Remember, too, that you can follow the rules and still have your own values, set your own style and timetable, pick your own places, companions.

DO YOUR OWN PLANNING AND PREPARATION

If I ever had the nerve to jump out of an airplane at 5,000 feet, I'd want to pack my own parachute, because I know how much the outcome depends on how, when, and for that matter **IF** that chute works on the way down.

In life, we all do a lot of jumping out into space and into places and situations we've never been before. The only way to have any control and confidence is to be as well prepared as we can be for what's coming—and who knows what this means, in most cases, as well as we do? How much we're likely to eat, drink, sleep, and sweat on the way, how much we can lift and tolerate, how well we can see and hear, what our allergies are, what we can't do without. Who we want to travel with. Don't let "**they**" decide for you and just anyone

pack your chute. You don't know if it would be a Friday afternoon or a Monday morning chute, if "they" did it drunk or drugged or fully sober. Do your own planning, don't depend on "they" (committees, the folks, bosses, past history or statistics, spouses) to do it for you.

"Committees" are poor planners— they're fine for reviewing and maybe readjusting things, but a bad source of the original planning and preparation. You need to do it yourself, tailoring the trip to fit your talents, temperament, energy, and level of commitment. Because when someone else packs your lunch, suitcase, briefcase, or diaper bag, then when it's time to eat, dress, or address the project, you have to get by with what's there. Whether it's what you needed or wanted or not, whether it works or not—that's what you've **got**! I see thousands of hazy-eyed high school students asking others "What do you think I should do for a living? Where should I work? What shall I study?" Getting input and advice is good, but letting people actually organize, plan, and prepare for you, choose your direction for you, can be crippling, like letting someone buy your shoes.

Do your own planning. Use others' ideas and checklists if they help, but make your own adaptations of them, scan your own brain and then pack your own bag. That's one big secret of being highly productive.

LISTS

I have lists, I use lists, I love lists, but lists don't make you do anything. They don't change anything, they don't inspire, don't speed you up or slow you down, they don't organize you much either. They're just a record so you won't forget what you have to do. It's just like a grocery list: it taxes your memory less if you have things down there, can see them, then check them off. If you start expecting a list to save or discipline you, to prioritize your life and assignments, to make you reach goals simply because you've listed them—forget it, Fred. It'll be your downfall.

Likewise, don't take the order on lists too seriously. Remember a few years ago when the president of some big Fortune 500 company had the answer for accomplishment? "Just make a list. Put the most important things on the top and don't go on to number two until number one is done." This is one of the most anti-productive approaches I've ever heard of, and I wasn't surprised to hear that he later bankrupted the company he managed.

What if something critically needed to accomplish #4 on the list was missing, so you got hung up there for a couple of days? What about those new things that crop up about an hour after you've made the list, and they still need to be done? You prioritize to the situation, not the list.

Let's look at an example of this. You have two seemingly similar secretaries. They have the same general abilities and education, however one is efficient and does okay, the other is effective and does phenomenally. Why? It's their approach to listing. Both have lists and both have schedules and duties for the day—then (as it always will) some surprise thing comes up, something unimportant. The efficient secretary adds it neatly and logically to her list of things to do, after the last thing she listed this morning. The effective secretary scans her list, looks at the new chore, and places it wherever it will get done the fastest and the best. She ignores **order and protocol, the clock, and previously established priorities,** because maybe doing it right then will only take five minutes and if she waits until later, till its logical place on the list, it will take two hours.

No great accomplisher or producer ever operates with a rigid list—it will throttle freedom and flexibility.

Who's Afraid of the Big Bad List?

As for the size of your list of "To Dos," the bigger, the better! Don't hesitate to put it all down, even the impossible dreams and the know-I-can't-get-to-it-yets. Low producers always list and consider and work from the practical. Real movers start with the **possibilities** and cut them down to the practical.

If you start with a list by focusing first on the practical, you will eliminate some of the wonderful possibilities you have in you. At one time I had over 6,000 To Do's on my list, and several thousand of them are done now, too. It's heartening to be-lieve and know that a man or woman is capable of doing not a mere 6,000 things, but an unlimited number. The more the merrier, and the more there are, the better position you'll be in to change jobs to fit your mood and momentum. If you elimi-nate things from your list, both you and they lose a chance at the time slot that will always pop up in a down time, or the spaces that come along every day when we least expect them. Just quit trying to fit a time to every To Do, instead let them

15 MINUTES...
15 DAYS...
15 YEARS..

STUFF TO DO

slide into the time in your life they might happen to fit.

I'd even distribute, publish, or hang up my lists for others to see. One of the best ways to get things done is to make your path public, then others will jump in and help you and you can help others.

The best list wisdom I know is **carry your list with you at all times.** Keep it in plain sight or accessible, and **look at it often**!

Which Priority Takes Precedence?

I'm often asked how one can master the art of juggling priorities, know which "need to do this NOW" is #1, when you're being pulled and pressed in all directions. This has nothing to do with ability, I assure you, you already have the ability. The real battle here is values. If you have a clear direction in what you're doing, priorities are a mere matter of selecting and organizing your activities for the day. If you're having prob-lems with priorities, you better examine (or reexamine and reaffirm) **where you are going and why.** Once that's figured out, your priorities will be too.

Make Sure It's Worth the Time

For many years my company has con-tracted the cleaning and maintenance of public pay stations (phone booths!). Simple as these units are, there are several levels of service you can give them. The first is what we might call the "lick and promise" level, and it would only take about five minutes and cost $2.00 per booth, but it would be unsatisfactory. The other ex-treme of maintenance, the "gold plate" level, would take at least an hour and cost $15 or $20 a booth. Even if you could afford it, the gold plate going-over wouldn't make sense because of the rapid deterioration from weather and use. A middle-level job, a good commercial cleaning, would take about 15 or 20 minutes. It would keep the booths clean, fresh, and pleasant to use, and only cost about $5.00 each. Going further than that and polishing all the outside metal, plastic, and glass to dia-mond brilliance would be a waste of time, because within hours the finish would oxidize, waterstain, and be handprinted all over and look no better than the less expensive commercial job which serves the purpose. Gold-plating would take four times as long and cost four times as much and really benefit no one.

The same is true of washing a car or sweeping a floor. One minute after the job is finished, dust, dirt, crumbs, and pollution begin to build up again. It would be pretty silly to start over to resweep the floor or rewash the car the minute you finish, because a reasonable level of cleanliness will do, and is what we're really after.

In all of your projects, think this through and **allocate your time according to the value of the undertaking.** Standards are a pivotal part of any project, and you have to pick yours if you are going to be a producer.

Reverse Those Little and BIG Projects

We seldom have anything "medium" to do. Once we've settled on a direction our projects, chores, and goals seem to be either big or little ones and we shape and engrave them in our mind that way. Then 99% of us have the impulse to attack, work on, and finish at least 44 little ones before getting at the big one. It's a kind of an avoidance ailment. Even if the big one is far more important (which it usually is), we warm up to, prepare ourselves for, and stay immersed in the little ones, and as we do that big one looms over us ever and ever more menacingly.

Why do we do it? Big does usually mean more work and more commitment and a loss of some of our flexibility to leave work early. But the real reasons run deeper. Big projects usually involve some big-picture thinking (which like most stretching, we automatically avoid). They often involve some **change** as well, so we want to put them off as long as possible. And the risks are bigger with big projects, we aren't so sure that we'll succeed with them.

So we love the little things and avoid the big ones... it seems easier. But the opposite is actually true. Doing the big project first is generally not just faster, but easier on us mentally and physically. The price—in time, money, guilt, worry, trouble, and delayed progress—of even one big project undone weighs us down every day of our lives, through every one of those little projects we keep doing to avoid the big one.

Big doesn't always mean long, either. One of the greatest mistakes we all make in production is in putting off those one-day jobs or projects that will bless and affect our whole life from that moment

forward, yet we dodge them, keep transferring them from list to list, even for five or ten years.

Just for fun, do a reverse. For a month, forget the little projects (keep them on a list somewhere, but don't do any of them or even think about them). Instead, tackle a couple of the major projects that you've pushed ahead for a while now. You'll have the immediate satisfaction of dealing with some big overdue issues. And by the time you finish those big projects you'll notice that many of the little ones on your list will be gone, automatically sandwiched in with or solved by the big one.

With a bit of practice you can always take advantage of this, the fact that most big projects have pockets of time in which you can do little projects at the same time. Being involved in one thing doesn't mean we have to forego doing anything else. Direction can have a thousand paths to its destination.

SCHEDULING

The word has a fascination for the time management generation, but you really don't have to know much about scheduling to get a lot done. I dislike schedules myself, they come on rather like an appointment with the hangman.

Schedules will bind and stiffen you if you follow them too close. So much time is wasted, for example, when something that's been scheduled is canceled because of rain or illness or whatever. Everyone loses at least half a day spinning their wheels and mentally retooling themselves. Scheduling also has a way of inhibiting ambition and action—it shifts our brain out of "what if" gear.

Good scheduling is having a big frontlog (see p. 70) and then rolling with the flow, not being controlled by the clock or the calendar.

My wife and I, for example, purchased some property on Kauai (the garden isle of Hawaii) and started a long term-project of designing and building a maintenance-free house. One winter we squared away our personal and business affairs and left for Hawaii for a while. I took some manuscripts and new book ideas and a list of forty other things to do in the two months we planned on staying—gardening and landscaping work, visiting with our many friends there, and building our house were the main objectives. There was no predetermined order or attempt to put things into time slots on my list, it was just a list of objectives. The first morning was sunny and we really went for it, unscheduled, out into the yard and had a ball whaling away at weeds all day. We didn't stop to eat at regular times, just worked on the task to our hearts' content. We did the same the next day, started feeling "in shape," and decided that this might be a good plan for the next five days. We didn't schedule it but we did prepare for it.

Then the rains came—rain like you've never seen. Our house is six miles from Mt. Wiaialiai, the wettest spot on earth (600 inches of rain a year). For three days, nonstop rain all day and night. I selected (totally unscheduled) one of the book topics, the one that fit my mood and in four days drafted a book. About that time I received a call from a national TV network producer who offered me a slot as a regular guest, and wanted some help with segment ideas. I took two or three days then and wrote up the scripts (totally unscheduled). I even left for New York for a couple of days. Two more phone calls alerted me to other important activities and I rolled them right into my week and went on. Fun, fast, and exciting. If I'd been following a "schedule" I would only have accomplished about half of what I did, and I'd have been constantly caught up in the confusion of rescheduling.

Rigid scheduling is usually unproductive.

A sales manager proudly showed his boss the scheduled contacts and sales for the month ahead. A wall chart covered with bright pins showed where each objective and salesman was. "What do you think?" he asked the boss. "I think," said the boss, "scheduling is taken care of—now if you want to see action I'd suggest you take those pins out of the map and stick them in the salesmen."

Day Dedication

As for setting aside or budgeting a day or a **block of time** for a certain project—careful, careful, top producers don't do it that way.

"I'm going to use Tuesday morning to sign the papers on the new place." If you block or schedule or set aside that time for it, you'll stretch it out and use up that much time whether you actually need it or not. You can spend a whole day on the closing or more realistically spend two hours, depending on how much of a ceremony you want to make out of it.

Often, too, jobs we dread, or that aren't quite our cup of tea, become magnified in our mind, so we overestimate how much time will be required for them. There was a giant pile of press clippings, for example, in a corner of the office for the longest time, because everyone shuddered at the thought of how long it would take to sort and file them all. When someone finally faced up to it, three years' worth of accumulation and dread (which we imagined would easily take two days to deal with) was disposed of in **two hours**. If we'd blocked out two days for this, we'd probably have used them.

Or you may run into the opposite problem with your preselected block of time—it turns out to be too small for the project slotted there, so you end up deep in guilt and a chain reaction of block reshuffling and reassignment and apologies.

Designating days or certain stretches of time for jobs is a real weakness of low producers, a limiting approach and a confession of not being able to control more than one thing at a time.

The fun of life is beating the clock, not letting it regulate you and your projects. Do all you can, as fast as you can—and don't get too hung up on WHEN.

SHOULD I DO IT IN ORDER? (NOT ALWAYS)

One of the biggest struggles people have with direction is that it might "reduce their freedom, thwart creativity, dampen thrills, offer no flexibility," etc. Not so! Direction is only a committed choice, a goal, a chosen route or course, not a strait jacket. If on the way someone burns your bridges, you hit a storm, or run out of steam, you have 110 options to go under, over, around, or through to reach your goal. The only important part is to keep holding course to the lighthouse you are heading for. Direction isn't a total allegiance to any order, not a stern, unyielding system. Direction may need to be an undeviating course but it isn't a straight rigid line. Just watch super producers, the ones with shiny 48-hour watches, work.

Should we start with #1, for instance, then go to #2, work from top to bottom, front to back? When I filmed a TV ad in New York, and we shot the end of the story first, the middle second, and the beginning last, it was confusing at first because like the rest of you I'd learned to go "in order." But as it turned out, it went twice as fast flip-flopping around like this.

There are no hard and fast rules for an efficient order of completing things. Order is often how something best organizes itself, not how we organize it.

That's why high producers don't like to have too many people involved in their activities, because they can't always chart the exact number of people they'll need, or plot the exact sequence or order of things. If the mood hits them, they get in a rhythm or on a roll, they may shoot off in what seems like an entirely different direction (holding course with their overall directional setting, all the time). They'll jump around on projects or change something right in the middle of the most important part. And they often establish order **during,** not before!

COURSE CORRECTION

One of my teammates was pitching his best game ever. He'd held the other team to a standstill and was cruising through the last inning, with a runner on first. As he began his next pitch, his windup knocked his hat down over his eyes, instantly eliminating his view of the entire field, including the batter he was throwing to. As you may know, once a pitcher has started to throw to a batter he can't stop the motion. If he does, it is a "balk," and the runner can

AT LEAST I DIDN'T BALK.

advance a base. The balking rule came immediately to my friend's mind and so he proceeded to throw the ball blindly (but softly) in the direction of the batter. The batter, of course, slugged the life out of the ball and the runner, instead of getting one base, got all bases and the ball game.

In "made an error" situations like this we usually have more time to think things through than this pitcher did. But too often, even so, because we are already in motion and rolling, we let a simple course correction become a crash.

It is a hard thing to do, stop and adjust things, taking some loss of time or progress in the process. But course correction, when it's needed, is the wisest of all courses for a fast mover. It may feel like backtracking but it isn't, it's just getting back on track, and it saves a lot of time in the long run.

I remember once visiting a Fuller Brush plant with a reputation of making magnificent, high-quality brushes. Off to one side, I saw a whole barrel full of beautiful wood handles. It looked like a trash can, and when I asked I found out that indeed it was. I lifted out some of those fine polished handles on their way to being made into

sawdust and moaned. I could barely find a blemish on them. The workers there told me that it was hard at first to dispose of something, or completely redo it, because of one little flaw or weakness. But at the end of the line where other parts and the reputation of 10,000 other brushes had to depend on the strength and quality of the one, then it made sense.

I've done things like this myself. You're putting in a big beam, even welding one into a building, and pausing for a moment to check your progress, you notice that it's a little crooked. No way do you want to stop, pull it out, and redo, but considering the fact that you otherwise will be building on a crooked base, realignment only makes sense.

This is the toughest discipline of all for me, stopping the momentum of a great work to correct a tiny error.

Good producers do it. Your 48-hour clock can afford it.

"YOU CAN'T SERVE TWO MASTERS"?

That is true, but it's talking about allegiance and direction, not duties. When it comes to simply tasks, you can serve two masters, or ten or a hundred at the same time. I've seen one person have twenty-two tops going at once, fifteen kites flying. I've seen people play five instruments at the same time, and innovative fishermen tending thirteen rods. And thousands and thousands of farmers grow a half-dozen different crops at the same time.

If you make an activity your master, you can only serve one at a time. If you stay the master, you can multiply at will. We all

THOSE DIRECTION DISTRACTIONS ALONG THE WAY

You want to do more and better, you want more time. The gang of time thieves you have to contend with includes overdoing, overdebating, and failing to go all the way and commit yourself. All of these thrive in an atmosphere of little or no direction.

OVERKILL

Is like stepping on an ant sixteen times to be sure you've got him. **Over** anything generally undoes the objective—overeat, overheat, overload, over pack, over speak, over clean, over buy, over stay.... There's plenty of overkill in doing, too.

A man and wife in our community, for example, were assigned a ten-minute talk each for a church meeting. The moment they accepted, everything else in life went on hold for the next two weeks. They spent hours and hours studying and preparing, all for a simple ten-minute talk. An informal presentation like this just isn't worth two weeks of work, there isn't a balance there. That much preparation wasn't necessary, even if they had the time. And unfortunately, the experience would probably keep them from accepting again, so they'd never have a chance to learn to do it faster and better. Ten talks like that and they'd be preparing them in ten minutes.

Human relations are important to us all, but even social niceties can be overdone. My Varsity Contractors is a pretty

play multiple roles simultaneously—we're a husband, uncle, brother, brother-in-law, cousin, grandparent, lawyer, president, ballplayer, fisherman, lover, repairman, painter, etc., all at the same time. We can even multiply the clock dial and get a 48-hour day out of it!

Because one thing is going on doesn't mean everything else has to stop. You don't watch a tree grow after you've planted it, that's nonproductive. You plant hundreds of things and with some nurturing they will grow on their own and you can be doing other things at the same time. I started a cleaning museum several years ago, and have a pretty nice collection now although I haven't spent much time "collecting." While doing other things, speaking, traveling, calling, writing, visiting, I'd mention it to people and tell them what I was looking for and how enthused I am about the project, asking them to spread the word, too. In time things started to come in, and they've kept on coming. "When did you do that" someone will ask, "Oh, last year." "But you weren't here much of last year...." "So?"

big company now, and across my desk every so often come cards for the birthday or wedding of some staff member, and I sign them and route them on down the line. A while ago one came, and it was a thank-you card thanking us for sending a card. Can you believe it, a thank-you note for a thank-you note we had sent, and it had been through **ten departments already**! If I hadn't stopped it, there would have been fifty departments thanking them for thanking us for thanking them.

Likewise, I did a good deed for a woman while on a road trip once. It cost me nothing and helped her tremendously and I felt good about it. A week later came an elaborate thank-you note and some goodies, so of course I wrote back a thank-you note for her goodies. Now she sent me some pictures of her family and asked, would I please send them back after I had a chance to look them over, and I did. Then she sent me another thank-you note for sending them back. At least one more round followed this, and I have tons of mail to answer every week!

Things like this can get to be kind of like the bowing routine in Japan—you should bow back after someone bows at you. If two people think that way, it's going to be a day of bowing.

A well-directed person can often do a half-dozen projects while their counterpart is overkilling on one. Things worth doing aren't always worth doing well, sometimes getting the job done is enough! Overkill (we've all done this while sanding something) is going on and on in an activity until it slips over from a positive to a negative, and even starts damaging the result. Even useful productive things became nonproductive when they're **overdone**. Learn to cut off activities when your inner instinct tells you they're finished.

Overkill can be cured simply and easily by always knowing where and what the finish line is, having good direction before you start. "Stop" and "done" are easy to see, if you look before you leap into an activity. So decide what the finish point is, and no matter how things are going when you get there, stop. Get another bucket if you must, but don't run the one over. Overkill is a waste of time and money and usually a pain to the recipient, too, the one we intended to please with all that extra effort. Find out before you start beating something to death, how dead it has to be and work until you're there and then move on.

LETTING ANALYSIS OVERWHELM ACTION

On a business trip, I got to flipping the dial on the hotel TV one night and there were a total of 22 channels—17 of them hard at work analyzing, projecting, hashing and rehashing. What could happen? And what if it did? What might happen if the present trend continued? What could have happened instead of what did happen? Not one solid bit of actual reality. No wonder it takes an hour and a half to watch sixty minutes of this stuff.

In the sports and political arenas, people spend hours, months of their time on polls and predictions which don't change anything or mean a thing until the game is played or vote is held, then the answer will be clear. Rehashing past events will never change the outcome of games or political gains, either. It's pretty dumb unless you're an analyst who is getting paid to make predictions.

Nonproducers are always reporting, analyzing, evaluating, discussing, mourning what has happened or might happen instead of making things happen. They're always kicking through the ruins of the fire speculating, instead of cleaning it up and starting a new building. They spend hours of time and energy every day discussing what might have been, had whomever done whatever instead of what they did. Second guessing like this has no value and can change nothing. Meddling, opinionating, and deciding for other people will only cut into your own fun time and progress... getting into the affairs of others will only keep you from go-getting.

Don't sit around waiting for the media or your favorite social group to tell you how things are, have been, and will be. Few real producers hang around and collect statistics. That just corrals your creativity and lines you up instead of letting you set your own lines. Your goal is to **make your own statistics!**

DELAYED DECISION-MAKING

Indecisive people are never high producers. Learning to make decisions once and for all, not with "maybe," or "I'll see," but a resounding one-time "I will" has to become part of your vocabulary and conduct. More and more of us are having our

direction set and our decisions made for us by the company, the boss, the government, the county, the city, the counselor—even well qualified and educated people just coast along. It's easier, safer, and handier to let someone else decide, then go along with it and see what happens. There's lots of name and job protection in letting others do the deciding.

AFTER CONSIDERABLE CONSIDERATION AND QUITE A BIT OF CONTEMPLATION I'VE DECIDED TO MAKE A DECISION!

The decision to get into the action is the first and foremost stumbling block for most of us.

You can't just educate yourself into high production. The moment of decision to practice the principles, instead of just learn more about them, has to come. Some training and even inspiration is often necessary and it isn't time wasted... for a while. But the **decision** to do it is where the ball game really starts, all the rest is practice, it doesn't count.

So make that decision, and mean it, like:
I'm never going to break training
I will be on time
I will work ten hours a day for the next year

The biggest battle of go-getting is **over** the minute you decide to stop brooding and stalling and wondering and philosophizing and analyzing, and just DO the job at hand. Trying it out, thinking about it, considering it, won't accomplish anything except confusion and discouragement. Doers decide and do, the average person can't even decide to decide. And so they remain... still average. Confined to, but not content with, a 24-hour (or less) day.

Most of us have the equipment and power to travel well in life, however few of us do, because we won't commit to a direction and get started on it. It's like our automobile—if we leave it in neutral, we can rev the motor full blast, burn a lot of gas, make a lot of noise, and wear the motor out, but never move. And when you don't move, people will:

run over you!
push you!
pull you!

...where **they** want to go, not where you intended or wanted to go!

Decision does put you at risk to a degree, but have you noticed all the high producers and go-getters, the big accomplishers you want to be like, are willing to take the risk?

"How did you get so successful?..."
"Good judgment."

"How did you get good judgment?..."
"Experience."

"How did you get experience?..."
"Bad judgment."

Confidence only comes from conquering. How do you get lots done? You decide, and then grab and handle the problem or the demand. Even if you foul it up a few times before you get it right, you are producing or on the road to production, something that can't be done just on the planning board or in a dream.

For the next week or so, watch the go-getters when a situation arises. They will react to it, stew, storm, or smile about it, hesitate for a moment or maybe a few minutes, and then make a decision—This is what we will do, or what I am going to do. They aren't saying it will be perfect or guarantee instant success or results, just "This is what I will do." After they say it, amazing things happen. Even if the decision was dead wrong, somehow they surge ahead and end up with a good score.

Notice how no one ever gives much help to indecisive people? How can they, if they don't know where you're headed? Once you decide everyone jumps in and helps, some may even jump in and criticize and fight you, but all in all there is action and progress, and something productive is in the making!

An old farmer I know said "When you get started, you're half done" and that old fellow had it figured out. Think about your own life. How many times have you dreaded doing something—put it off, avoided it, sidestepped it thirty times, burned up acres of energy worrying about it, analyzed it for hours on end. Then once you decided and jumped in, it took only hours to complete or pull off. First you were flooded with relief, then the second wave came, "Gadfrey, I could have done this four years ago and saved weeks of my life."

Think of all the people you know, and the difference between those who've never done anything wrong because they never took a chance, never risked or tried anything, and those who step out ahead of everyone else. People don't cheer till one of the horses breaks out of the pack and surges ahead—when they all run together in a big dust cloud it doesn't rattle anyone's emotions. Even the failures who venture forth and expand their life are more loved and interesting than those who just stay holed up. When we lengthen our stride, magnify our calling, we not only find the 48-hour day but end up blessing other lives along with our own.

DOERS DON'T TRY, THEY DO

We have a poster here in our office that says:

> *"If you ever use the word 'try' around here... you are automatically fired!"*

Listen to top producers—you'll seldom or never hear the word "try." How would you react to a pilot who told you he was going to try to fly the plane you were on? Or the surgeon who just before important surgery told you "Well, I'll **try**." Or the boss who promised to **try** and pay you for your work, or a waitress who said " We'll **try** to get the food to you." I had an appointment in New York once and the host of the program involved told me, "I'll try to be there at 8:30, if I'm not catch a cab." Man, do I wait till 8:35 or what? When the word try is involved we don't know anything and we can't do anything. He needed to say either "I'll be there," or "Catch a cab."

When someone tells you "I'll try to get this done for you," what does that tell you... nothing! Even saying "I tried my very best" means nothing in life or production. Doers don't try, they do or they don't do. "Try" and "decide" can't be used in the same sentence!

RIGHT ROADS
RIGHT IN FRONT OF US

As wandering scholars of the past collected answers to "the secret of life," most of us today in our multi-pull society are wandering in rather desperate search for the secrets of getting more done. We don't want a fountain of youth near as bad as a "fountain of doooth!"

Over the years I've compiled my own little list of secrets, picked up along the way from my own experience, and from talking to the mountain movers of today and watching them operate. These ideas aren't new, in fact they are so available, common, and free that we often overlook them in our grasping for something profound to set our clock and compass by.

1. Obey your own experience and instinct! Follow your first impulse. Without any conscious effort, we all come up with a sound and efficient course of action for ourselves. We are born with this "automatic transmission" of the mind. Learning to follow these feelings requires some experience, some humility, and some discipline, but it's a wonderful way to set your compass. So listen to the inner ticking that talks to you. The wisdom and promptings of the spirit inside us are a gift we all have that we don't use enough. Follow it, it works!

2. Believe history. Too often our main interest in history has been to get a grade from it or be box-office entertained. Yet nothing is plainer and more accurate than a simple look at the record to see how millions of others made out with their direction. Wouldn't we be dumb to repeat the actions of those who ran off the road or walked off the cliff? Governments are too cumbersome and slow to learn from history, but as individuals we can get pure, truthful intelligence from it. And we can pick the 48-hour day people of the past to pattern our own lives after. But few do it.

3. The Scriptures. Our track record is still far short of our creator's, still experimental compared to the expertise of the inspired. The scriptures can keep you out of the whistle-stop stations on your journey, focus you on the best, most promising landing places. I've studied masterminds at the universities, weighed their logic and observed their destiny. Most of their infallible logic has ended up a guess compared to the scriptures, which have shown with time to have a scary accuracy of outcome.

4. Wise People. Not smart, but wise people. Those who lived and produced wonderment during "their time," for example, knew a lot about time. What they did and how and why they did it is worth copying. Don't parrot a personality, just pattern a procedure, maybe readjust your route to match one they used to do something faster and better. This is kind of like following "individual history."

TIME TO TAKE A BREAK

TIME TO TAKE A BREAK and refresh ourselves on **why** we want to do more. Sure, it's fun, rewarding, and profitable. But there are a couple of other very good reasons to do it.

- **Public relations**—selling yourself and your causes, purposes, wants, and needs to others is another big key to keeping all your goals and projects headed toward accomplishment. Doing a lot puts out lots of broadcast fodder on its own.

- It's good **communication**! Yes, this word communication is so overused we are all sick of it as the ultimate success formula. But being in touch with others is a big key to higher life quality and doing does that automatically for you. If you do more you'll never have to say "communication" again.

- For **social security.** No, not a reserve of cash to be disbursed later, but a reserve or carryover of something to do... later. Having nothing to do someday, or not being needed someday, is indeed a fate worse than death, it is torture. 48-hour days create quite a reserve, you have hundreds of handles. And little idle time for dying.

CHAPTER FIVE

The Magic of Early

Answering the question I'm most often asked, "How do you get so much done in a day, Don?" I've accumulated lots of notes, essays, stories, and sayings. So when putting this book together I proudly pulled out all this material, pawed through it, pasted it together, and ended up with two big chapters of "plan your work and work your plan" and "preparedness is precious" stuff. You've seen or heard similar in magazines, books, and seminars. The manuscript was finished and polished and had been read and liked by some publishers; I had lots of money invested in it by now. Then on my last reading, I ripped those two chapters out, saving you some reading!

I was convinced there had to be a bottom line, a shorter, quicker, easier, if not near perfect way to say the same thing in ten pages or less. I went over and over all my systems, techniques, tools, and outlines. Nothing profound popped up besides the usual "hard work, persistence, followup"—all those familiar success keys which we change the names of every year or so. I never did find the "secret" of my 48-hour performance until sitting in an executive committee meeting of my cleaning company one day. I was listening to the bosses report all the recently developed problems throughout the eighteen states we operate in. As I listened, I began to jot a one-word reason or summary beside each. I found myself writing late, **late, behind, late, forgot, late**.

Then that evening at a friend's house, a panic phone call regarding a school deadline assignment came in—the reason again, late. In the headquarters of a mail order company the next morning I eavesdropped on ten incoming calls and the scrambling around and apologizing that followed—five of the ten calls were the result of LATE.

I don't live with late so it hadn't occurred or appeared as the villain of the day to me. Just to double-check then I ran over to my corporate office and asked eleven key executives—CPA's, safety officers, managers, etc.—what percent of their calls and correspondence that day had to do with problems. "65%," was the answer. What was their one-word summary of the cause for most of those problems? You guessed it, people being late. One "late" situation generated three calls and two extra pieces of paper, etc.

I had it! The most important principle of the 48-hour day, the "solve most" word in the vocabulary of accomplishment. I had the two chapters replaced with two words.

BE
EARLY

The early bird got much, much, more than the worm.

1. She got the first choice of morsels.
2. She got the admiration and respect of the other birds.
3. She got good press and publicity.
4. She got "no sweat" comfort and relaxation.
5. She got the rest of the day to do anything she wanted.

While all the late birds hunted, dug, scratched, fought, lined up, negotiated, made excuses, prayed, hoped, crowded, and shoved.

Just look what EARLY eliminates.

If you don't do anything else I recommend in this entire book, read and follow these next few pages. The simple, inexpensive principle of being early will single-handedly, automatically, for no cost and little effort, prevent about 80% of your "time management" and personal and organization problems. And increase your quality of life a wonderfully predictable amount.

Being early in life carries a competency flag with you. It waves to all the world a message that you can be depended on. Late, on the other hand, is like dragging a ball and chain, rumbling to all that you are always bringing up the rear and cannot totally be trusted to be there, no matter how good a person you may be.

Victor Borge's famous comment in concert about

sums it up. He was well into his performance when a woman came in late, fighting her way through the rows to her seat near the front. Borge stopped playing and as she proceeded—trampling over people, embarrassing, rustling, and disturbing her way to her seat—he said (much to her chagrin, as all eyes focused on her ill-timed arrival) "Excuse me, excuse me, excuse me." After she sat down, he walked over near where she was sitting and said, "Where are you from, Ma'am?"

"Fifty-Seventh Street," she said.

"Well, Lady, I'm from Denmark and I was here on time."

People are much more irritated by late than we ever know, it can dampen everything from promotions and raises to sexual desire. Late people crowd us, physically and mentally, all the time. We all hate the fact that their lateness undoes our schedule and disrupts our day. Showing up late for work or sending something in late, no matter how well done, still means a mark against you.

WHEN TO PREPARE? EARLY!

There's no such thing as too far ahead. I have speeches, appointments, and projects scheduled for 1996 through 1998, and though this is only 1995, as soon as the times and the topics are set, I start preparing for those presentations and projects, collecting notes and ideas. I do it over the course of the year, it takes almost zero time, and I end up with a choice speech or whatever with little time or cost in it. If I waited until the night or even the week before, then

I'd have to spend hours hunting, making calls, and sitting down and studying. When you spread it out over time, the work almost does itself, and better!

If I have a trip coming up, I never pack the night before, but set the trunk or suitcase out and drop things in it over the whole week ahead. That way I'm never in a last-minute rush, so I seldom forget anything, and I'm not up at midnight picking out my clothes and ideas the night before. My dad ran a ranch four times bigger than any of the neighbors' without any hired help. Now I realize why he was so good at it. We never went to bed one night without knowing exactly what we were going to be doing the next day, and without the tools for tomorrow lined up and laid out. Our equipment and machinery was ready six months before our neighbors', who waited until the very week they needed it, to check out the grain combine. Then if they needed a part it took weeks to get it, they lost sleep, crops, and schedules. We had plenty of lead time, so if we came upon a problem we were able to handle it easily.

Being ready in advance is sure fun and comforting. As a boy, one of my jobs was feeding the cattle. It took 15 minutes to muscle the bales up to the mangers, and only about three minutes to feed. I dreaded rounding up the bales, especially when I was in a rush. So right after the evening feeding, I'd round up the bales for the morning and place them right by the manger. This way if it was cold or windy, or I was running late or had a ball game, I could feed in three minutes instead of 18. Plus it always feels good to work in advance, to have something done ahead, ready, just in case.

WORK AHEAD, NOT BEHIND

Observe high producers, and you'll notice the word "later" seldom issues from their lips. Sure we do always have to fit something into our schedule and even the best producer still has moments of weakness, of not feeling quite up to doing something right now. Anything slated "to do later," however, is at great risk of ending up on one of those "unresolved" piles so many of us have in our lives. We've stacked this stuff in line to get to, but haven't gotten to it yet. It's kind of like putting things in a little fix-it or do-it hospital and then not attending to them. They just fill up all the beds in our brain and have to be fed and looked after to keep them alive. For sure they seldom heal themselves.

Most Later things end up taking more energy, aggravation, and worry than just doing them right away ever would. When a neglected 15-minute job goes stale it suddenly becomes a two-hour nightmare accompanied by unnecessary emotional wear and tear. Or consider the building inspector in our city who told the owners of a building to get the roof repaired. They had an estimate done and it came to $5,000. They didn't want to spend that much right then, so they waited two years. By then the water had ruined the walls, floors, doors, and the support beams. The fixing cost two years later was $50,000! The owners first saw the leak when it was $15 to fix… and waited.

Make working ahead and early your style, convert all those "later's" to now, which is ten times as efficient.

Being out and in front of and ahead of things is much more inspiring than always being behind, digging your way out. There is a whole different feeling to being the aggressor, looking ahead and doing ahead, rather than forever fighting and patching up problems that should have been handled a long time ago.

The time to get things done is when they can be done most quickly, cheaply, and enjoyably. That is almost always EARLY.

Toss "later" out of your vocabulary right along with the word try. Along with "LATER" we have to carry the vague burden of "when?" Even "see you later" has a negative and instantly built in "when?"

KEEP A FRONTLOG, NOT A BACKLOG

Ninety percent of people keep and use backlogs, lists of work to do, or things that should be done. Things to dig into when and if they get caught up with their daily list of things to do.

High producers don't have backlogs. When you work from behind you never really catch up enough to be able to go back and pick up. Producers maintain a **front**log, a list of things to do ahead. When you're always working ahead of yourself, pushing things ahead of you rather than pulling them along behind you, you have twice the control.

Just how do you assemble a frontlog? I can use one of those business buzzwords and tell you to be pro-active instead of reactive, or ask you to be active rather than passive, but telling people to "be" this or that is almost futile. Out of all the "Be's" preached and commanded and suggested, however, there is one truly easy and self-rewarding behavior. It is the indisputable Number One in learning to have a 48-hour day, as well as the exact way to create a frontlog. What is this biggest "BE" in the books of accomplishment? **BE EARLY**, of course!

Type up your frontlog and carry it with you always... even to church, to bed, and to the movies. Then make little swipes and snips at it as you can, as the mood strikes and opportunities small, medium, and large appear. If you keep chipping away at it like this consistently, gradually the original projects will be done and disappear, and fresh new To Do "twigs and branches" will appear on your log.

Remember, productive people always have a bigger list of things to do, not a smaller one, as life goes on, that's what makes having a 48-hour day worth it all.

WHAT TIME OF DAY IS BEST FOR DOING?

Another question I'm asked a lot is "What time of day is best for 'doing'?" There is only one right answer for me... EARLY.

For me, the morning hours will always outproduce the evening hours 3 to 1. I do all my finely tuned mental stuff such as writing in the wee morning hours. When my brain dies, I go to the office at noon and do executive work, calls and errands, letters, etc. When body and brain both die, I hit (in the early evening) the knuckle and muscle physical stuff, work with a pitchfork or shovel. Then I use the "overtime" (late) hours in the day to lay things out for the morning, so I can hit the road running and not thinking or hunting for a starting place.

This is, however, a strictly personal option. Decide and regulate this yourself, don't let me or anyone else (other than possibly your boss!) dictate the time of day in which you do most of your accomplishing. We might all use the same clock, but there are no rules as to which part of it we choose to use the hardest—it could be the left or right side or the bottom or somewhere in the middle.

Do keep other people's clocks in mind, though. Otherwise your project may come screeching to a halt because you need a part, supply, or consultation with someone who sticks with the old 9 to 5!

Some people jog in the morning and it stimulates them. It would just cut my edge and energy level. We're all different, so find a fit and follow it. **Your fit**—not any author's or consultant's—yours.

EARLY ELIMINATES DEADLINE STRESS

"Early" has the power to eliminate another ugly time stealer out of your life, deadlines. The word is seldom in a "do morers" vocabulary.

Deadline people are survivors, not doers. Deadlines are a crutch for the weak-willed and unmotivated. Deadlines eliminate all the joy of accomplishment as you're working for the deadline, not the completion of the project or task. People who diddle and ding with deadlines will ruin your nerves and work less efficiently than anyone around. Deadline people are the ones who invented and need Federal Express and overnight mail. Their habit of starting a day late instead of a day early cuts them out of any new or priority things that might come up by way of opportunity.

A deadline becomes your stalker the minute you set it, the name alone—"**dead-line**"—ought to tell you something. If you are early (no extra cost, no strain, no explanations) you don't have to worry about deadlines.

WAITING—GIVE IT A SHOT OF EARLY

The average American spends five years of his life **waiting**.

If you wonder sometimes why you can't seem to get much done, add up your time waiting not just in traffic but: to eat, pay, check in, check out, go to the bathroom, get the mail, catch a cab, be admitted, get what you ordered, actually be seen at your appointment with the doctor/lawyer, etc. Just about any attempt to do anything seems to get us caught up in some waiting time. So:

1. Avoid waiting situations whenever you can, by going **early** or at off times or not going at all. And whenever possible avoid people who keep you waiting every time.

2. Prepare, so you can use waiting time productively—carry some work (that you've prepared **earlier**) with you all the time. If you enjoy your work as you should, this is like carrying your tennis racquet around with you.

FIXING—DO IT EARLY

None of us are exempt from the need to fix things, but we do have a choice of when.

One of the rear tires on my seminar van was getting bald once, for instance. It almost cried out, "Change me! Change me!" as it went around—but I didn't fix it. I was holding out to maybe get just "one more trip" out of it. On the way to Los Angeles, deep in the heart of the Nevada desert, it blew—throwing too much weight on the other dual and it, a little worn, went also. Have you ever replaced tires at a "Last Chance Before Vegas" tire shop in the desert, or paid for a 75-mile tow? Not fixing that tire till later, cost over $500!

Likewise, a friend of mine had a butane tank with a leak—a tiny, tiny leak that he was going to fix later. Later was (as usual) longer than he thought and when fixing time forced itself upon him, the barbecue dinner was only half done and the butane had all leaked out. Now what would have only involved a 50¢ washer was a special trip to town (in a hurry), $19 worth of butane lost, and a picnicful of people with less respect for my friend.

Again here early comes to the rescue.

High producers learn to fix things when it's not only time to do so, but early. They don't wait for something to **make** them fix it, at the worst possible moment. You're going to have to deal with broken or non-working things sometime, for sure, **why not NOW, while they're in your court and control?** That's what the go-getters do.

To summarize and remind us of the power of early, I've included a couple of charts here.

MORE MAGIC OF EARLY

DAILY DETAIL	LATE	ON TIME	EARLY
LINES	stand and wait	stand in shorter line	no line
PARKING	walk 6 blocks/ pay a lot	fight other on-timers for the last two spots	you get the closest spot and can back your car in
A VISIT	no time left so just wave	a little "get-together"	a chance to really touch base
A BARGAIN	no bargaining power	average deal	a real bargain
CLEANING	have to let it go	time to wipe	time for those extra little touches
CHOICE	leftovers	already picked over by the early birds	first choice
PIT STOP	cross your legs	60% chance	take any stall for as long as you want
SEAT	fight-search-steal	take what they point you toward	choose what and where
TRAVEL	sweat and hurry	accomplish your objective	do a half-dozen little extras on the way
ASPIRIN AND DEODORANT	use plenty	just the standard amount	seldom need either one
EMERGENCY	worsens stress, risks, and problems	anxiety, risk, problem	you are calmer and in a better position to solve the problem
MENU	others have ordered for you	quick read	thoughtful selection
WEATHER	it has the upper hand	it dampens the situation	you have time to take steps to counteract it
TRAFFIC	use horn	have to go slower	no problem
ANXIETY	intensified	normal amount	less or none
PAPERWORK	increases	a drag	reduced
REPORT OR OTHER ASSIGNMENT	lower grade or black mark, even if the paper is excellent	met the requirement	time to pursue new thoughts or leads, no deadline stress
INJURY OR MEDICAL PROBLEM	prolonged pain, possible infection or permanent damage	stop or reduce pain and damage	prevent pain and damage
A BILL	dunning calls and letters, interest charges and penalties	meet obligation	improve credit rating, impress others, may get discount
PEST CONTROL	problem insect, bird, animal multiplies, does lots of damage	stop damage and annoyance	prevent damage and annoyance
HIRING	whoever's at hand	best of who's available now	time to find THE best
TIME EXCHANGE RATE	10 minutes late takes one hour from you	even exchange	10 minutes ahead gains you an hour

73

YOUR TIMING TALKS FOR YOU

What do you want to say with your life? Just about all of your plans and projects, and ultimately your reputation, will be affected if not controlled by which column you choose here. As you can see, I believe that even "on time" is late.

LATE says	ON TIME says	EARLY says
I'm not interested	Okay—expected (yawn)	I'm really interested
I'm not ready	Okay—expected (yawn)	I'm ready
I'm behind	Okay—expected (yawn)	Ahead
I'm uncomfortable	Okay—expected (yawn)	Comfortable
I have no confidence	Okay—expected (yawn)	Confident
I'm desperate	Okay—expected (yawn)	Relaxed
I'm out of control	Okay—expected (yawn)	In control
I'm leaving a lot to chance	Okay—expected (yawn)	I have a choice
I'll take whatever's left	Okay—expected (yawn)	I get what I want
I don't care about others	Okay—expected (yawn)	I care about your feelings
I'm buried	Okay—expected (yawn)	I'm on top of things
I'm a taker	Okay—expected (yawn)	I'm a giver
I'm preoccupied	Okay—expected (yawn)	I'm available
I can't make deadlines	Okay—expected (yawn)	I don't need deadlines
My style is "crisis management"	Okay—expected (yawn)	I plan ahead
I don't look beyond the moment	Okay—expected (yawn)	I look ahead
I'm a follower	Okay—expected (yawn)	I'm a leader
I have to be coerced	Okay—expected (yawn)	I can do it on my own
People snarl at me	Okay—expected (yawn)	People smile at me
This costs	Okay—expected (yawn)	This pays

Poor

Average

Excellent

74

FINALLY, you get to pick your label to live by. Be sure to pick one you'll be content to live with the rest of your life.

The Great Transformation Day

Lots of fully grown up folks still believe in the fairy godmother who, one of these days, will grant a magical change in our personal production. If we've attended enough training sessions, heard and memorized all the virtues of industriousness, one day (zap!) we will cross the line from poky to productive.

It's a fairy tale. The skills of exceptional production are gradually attained, not angel ordained. So don't get discouraged if you aren't seeing any magnificent transformations. The only change of habit or behavior that might yield anything close to this is changing over to being **early** in everything. The results of that particular transformation are pretty astounding—the rest of the 48-hour habits take practice and a while to ingrain themselves before they can guarantee you time blessings.

How About Some Help?

Seems like so many of the super doers we admire also have all the luck and talent or were born with a silver 48-hour watch on their wrist. **That's absolutely not true**. What is true is that they get more than their share of help and assistance.

High producers aren't lone wolves or one-man shows, as you might first imagine. In fact, they are the best team workers around. Big doers seldom do everything themselves as most people suspect. They need and get all the help they can, all the time. And their sources of it are simple and available to anybody.

Before sharing some of these aides of the high achievers, let's take a look at some "helps" that aren't such a big help.

FORGET ABOUT "THE BIG BREAK"

We always hear about that one great record-breaking feat, master move on the market, or "Hail Mary" pass, etc.—where a single event made a name or a million for someone. This is often referred to as "the big break." Lottery winners, ace pilots, speedway drivers are suddenly "somebody" all because they scored something newsworthy. We hear this enough that we start looking for the big moment or the break that will make us, or the day that our 48-hour watch will come in the mail from Ed McMahon. That's why so many people live disappointed lives. Never mentioned in the headlines are the rest of the facts:

1. The lottery player spent $10,000 on tickets before he won that million and 10 million other lottery players got nothing.

2. The pilot learned discipline and nerve milking cows and cutting trees as a teenager, had years of flight training, flew seventy missions, and was wounded three times and shot down twice prior to his big day. He was a good pilot **before** he shot down six enemy planes. That one act just made him visible.

3. The race car driver lost 167 races, was burned over thirty percent of his body once, and his passion for racing has cost him his life savings and three marriages so far. That one big win didn't begin to cover the costs.

Don't be deceived by "big breaks," they seldom, seldom come. This is even true of turning to the Lord. We read and hear of (and see on pray TV) such instant, dramatic conversions—it all happens in one big change of heart or emotional moment. The reality is that the average convert had more than a half-dozen small, casual, one-on-one contacts and often long rewarding experience with a member of that church prior to changing.

Whatever you do, don't waste your precious time and emotions gambling and praying and waiting for a big magical event triggered by someone else to put you on top. Don't live for the big light that is going to come on some day and make you rich, famous, secure, productive, and happy forever. That will only happen if you pick up many little sticks for a long time and build a big bright fire. Most accomplishment is the result of a lot of small or even tiny things added up over time. Don't save yourself for the spectacular, for the headlines. Score soundly in every game instead of dreaming of that one "forty point" night. Production always has a history, and **consistency** is what counts.

FORGET ABOUT "THE LEDGE"

Another big time waster is the search for the elusive "ledge." Once on life's road we only pick up speed, pick up loads and rules and responsibilities and opportunities and dreams, and more and more and more to do. Sooner or later it begins to get to us, and this is about when the idea of that "ledge" is formulated in our mind.

Somewhere... ahead... there is or will be a place, a ledge, a sanctuary, a rest stop, where we can leap out of the stream, jump off the merry-go-round. Time will stop there, and noises and demands too and we can just lie there for a while and pant and recover, catch up. After we've nursed our road wounds and calmly collected ourselves, we can do all that letter writing and meditation, complete all those undone chores and waiting projects. Then, all restored and rested, we can leap off the ledge and back into the fight of life, much the better now with no backaches or backlog.

Everyone has their dream of the ledge. Maybe it would be a minor injury that put us safely out of commission for a while so we can give ourselves all the time we need to catch up as we convalesce. Maybe it's a vacation, a spell in prison, being snowbound for a few months, any wild dream of a place to duck into and out of the sniping and lightning and milling of the everyday hassles and demands—making a living, caring for a home and family. We just need that little ledge—that release from the rat race—to stop and service our vehicles, to fix and heal and refuel.

Most of us are still looking and waiting for that ledge, as our salvation from society's demands and our crazy schedule and all those commitments, before they drive us insane or work us to death. There isn't a single one of us who hasn't been on the watch for it. In fact we anticipate it, with a great list of the things we are going to get done when we finally find or reach it.

I've been looking for mine since about the age of 21, and at 59 now, I finally realize that there ain't one! And anything I thought was one, wasn't—instead it was a road shoulder just loaded with more.

"Stopping to catch up" is unfortunately one of those idle wishes. How many of us ever (if we are actively engaged in a good cause) get time to stop? Few of us do, or will, and with each passing year it only gets harder to find stopping time to catch up. How many retired people have you

seen bragging about finally being caught up in life? They are usually clutching for more time as it slips by more frantically than any thirty- or forty-year-old. And even if you can manage to stop the clock, it probably won't aid your productivity. Most of the time when people do stop to catch up, they're so relieved to be stopped, they fall further behind.

The bottom line is, you are going to have to stay on the road and fix yourself **on** the road—en route, out in the open of the fast lane. You don't get to stop to get more done, you have to do it on the run, and you can. A 48-hour day can be your ledge.

YOU CAN'T RUN LONG ON STARTER FLUID (MOTIVATORS)

On those far below zero mornings on the Idaho ranch where I grew up, it was hard to get yourself going in the morning, and even harder to get the big tractors to go. Those cold engines often didn't have enough oomph to turn over. We couldn't risk the chance that they might not run, or that we'd run the battery down trying to get them started, so we had a fantastic little can of stuff called "starter fluid." A tiny bit of that in the piston chamber area would turn even a flicker of a spark into a running engine—just a quick spray into the carburetor and we'd be on our way. Dad would always caution us, "Not too much, just a bit, these engines can't run on starter fluid. Once they fire, the regular gas will take over." Indeed it did, and once the engine was warm it then started easily anytime during the day.

All of us who constantly seek a "motivator" to keep us going could take a lesson from this. You can't run long on motivators—stimulants, drugs, prizes, and other outside incentives for accomplishment. A motivator is like intravenous feeding, sometimes necessary to assure survival and progress, but if it continues too long it will cause weakness and damage. A motivator should only be used like Dad recommended for the starter fluid, "just a tiny bit." We don't run on motivators, and if we do, we'll need constant "fixes." And we'll fold when they run out, because like starter fluid, motivators are expensive. Motivators don't run anything, they simply help produce a spark that **may** turn into powerful continuous strokes of work.

Motivators may rouse us to accomplishment, but accomplishment is the sustaining reality. Once you build and produce, once your work results in something that changes a life, changes a structure, changes a direction, then it changes you, too, and feeds you just like a tank of fuel feeds a big engine.

DELEGATION WON'T DO IT ALL FOR YOU, EITHER

Is it a sure ticket to higher productivity, as so many seminar leaders tell us? The most fitting definition of this oversold "magic principle" of time management is this:

Delegation: an act that gives you the comforting illusion something is being taken care of, until you have time to deal with it yourself.

A couple of little glitches in delegation everyone forgets.

Delegation can be a way of doing more and better...

IF...

☐ you can afford to hire anyone to help, and the potential delegatee is:

☐ competent and responsible

☐ motivated and punctual

☐ and they understand, clearly and completely, what you want them to do

These four qualifications eliminate about 90 percent of the people you can delegate anything to. Delegation isn't an instant way out of management responsibility, or the cure-all solution it's constantly claimed to be—half of the stuff we're told to delegate, we could and should do ourselves. You can delegate a duty or task, but not the motivation and commitment to do it. You can delegate authority, but not your own accountability for how things turn out. What we really need is a course in distinguishing things that **can** be delegated, or intelligently assigned.

Some delegating can easily take longer than doing it yourself, by the time you choose someone, explain it all to them, and then check up and evaluate and keep quality control on what they're doing... and repair their mistakes. It doesn't make much sense to delegate out work you can do yourself, then spend three days following up on and disciplining the delegatee.

I had a volunteer supervisory job once over six buildings in six neighboring communities. It involved overseeing the cleaning of them, ordering the materials and equipment to do it, hiring, training, and supervising the custodians and determining their salaries, ordering fuel to heat the buildings, and doing repairs, painting, etc. as needed. And then making reports on it all. It appeared to be a big job, and although I was empowered to employ assistants, committees, secretaries, order clerks and other "people power" to make the job easier, I just did it all myself. I did the job for four years, and did it well. It took about **three hours a week** at the most, never derailed my schedule, and was really enjoyable. When a custodian wanted something I made myself available and talked it over with him or her for a few minutes, then took another five and personally wrote out the order and mailed it. I had the product sent to me, and on the way home or past one of the buildings I'd drop it off, visit with the staff, and inspect the building, lacing it in with other activities. I always knew exactly what was going on, and so could make my monthly reports in minutes.

When I moved out of the job, my replacement followed the organization's procedure manual and lined up assistants, helpers, order getters and all—and complicated the job about twenty times. When someone would call for an order he would take it, then call the order person, and they would order it. The product would be shipped to the building, and no one ever knew when (or if) it came in, so they had to make an inquiry into it, or call the order clerk to run it down. She would then hunt down and call the custodian, he would call her back, and so on and on down the "chain of command." When the monthly report had to be done, the whole process was even more complicated, and just locating and finding out things and calling people took a lot of time. Administrating took so much time, there wasn't even time to train, supervise, or clean! The job consumed **30 hours a week** and he hated it!

Too many people given leadership and management jobs think the whole idea is to get someone else to do all the work, including a professional assistant to hand out assignments. But a highly paid management job or running a team or home isn't a delegation job, it's a working, making it work job, where you do all you can yourself toward the goal, only assigning out a few things others can do more quickly and efficiently than you.

The natural urge to get off the firing line and let others take the brunt of the action is in all of us. But the fastest way to slow down productivity is to start removing yourself from the scene, from experiencing and facing and being part of what's going on. Being reported to, rather than being part of the report, will wean you from the real world fast, and ultimately you'll pay for it with time!

Let's move on to the real helpers now, and start with the best one—

YOUR FELLOW EVERYDAY MAN OR WOMAN (VOLUNTEERS!)

How do you get them to help? Well, you put up a sign:

- *I AM A NICE PERSON*
- *I NEED/WANT HELP*
- *IT IS GOING TO BE FUN...*
- *AND YOU CAN BE PART OF IT.*

Yes, most super doers have a sign exactly like this and they wear it 48 hours a day. Haven't you seen it on them? It is there and the reason it works so well is because everyone else sees it too, even though it is invisible.

This is how go-getters manage to recruit so much help. They make their path public. They aren't bashful about telling the world what they are up to: "This is what I'm going to do, and when and how and why." The average person is cautious and terrified about publicly charting the future (in case something goes wrong). High producers get people to lead for them, not just follow, by selling ahead.

People have an immediate attraction to well-directed people. They join with them in spirit and build a loyalty to them without even realizing it. This is because doers have a definite direction, a destination. They are going somewhere, moving, and any progress or action is exciting. The average person has been waiting for something like this and is grateful for it, willingly and enthusiastically contributes to it.

People love to be productively or even mischievously busy—they want in on, to be part of, "important goings-on."

This help from fellow humans is perhaps the most precious resource you will ever deal with, because it involves other people's lives and time. The doers that get the most help are usually unselfish. They don't hog all the fun and glory. So make sure your own sharing is regular and generous. Credit for accomplishments, praise, or profits—share them well.

HOW TO GET MORE DONE WITH OTHERS

The "do-morer" doesn't just turn things over to others, or join up with them. The doer holds the direction, the control. Because how you go about the "multi-person" type of project can make a tremendous difference in output and accomplishment. Let me give you an example of what I mean. Let's say you have to meet with others to discuss a project you will be undertaking together.

There are three basic possibilities here, in the very same setting and amount of time spent:

1. If you meet or begin and **neither of you** are ready, committed, or organized, has done much preparation and planning, you'll probably get something like a dozen worthwhile work-related exchanges, or transactions, made.

2. If the next time you get together **YOU**

really have the thing organized on your side, direction set, ideas and outlines written up, samples ready, sketches done, or whatever, and the other party/your potential helper is still totally unprepared, you'll still get almost double the amount of things done, compared to the first meeting.

3. If you meet and **both of you** are 100% clued in, organized, and prepared, you will achieve the ultimate of useful transactions, almost three times as many as the first meeting.

This is such a simple secret of getting more done with others, but it took me years to wake up to it. I'd always catch people at random, without warning, to get something done or going. Gradually I learned, when dealing with other people, that if I thought it over first, wrote it down, drew up some plans, etc., and came to them with a possible solution, not just a question or a problem, I got twice as much done. Then one day I realized that if I demanded the same of all the people who came to *me* half cocked, I could get even more done, better and faster.

Just do this for the next few weeks with everyone, at home and work, when they want to deal or go over something with you. **Tell them what to bring with them, why and where**, and watch your production go up and the amount of time it takes go down!

GROUPS—THE TWO-EDGED SWORD OF TIME CUTTING

Handling individual helpers is not too hard and not too risky, but having groups come to your aid can be spooky, a genuine two-edged sword when it comes to time cutting.

There are at least four sources of collective aid for your projects and undertakings:
1. Committees
2. Meetings
3. Seminars and courses
4. Associations

All of these can be lifesavers, but they can also choke and drain the life out of you. And use up your time.

If Moses had formed a committee, the Israelites would still be in Egypt.

Committees

Some marvelous works have come from committees, some great relationships have been built, new leaders tagged and tested, scattered brilliants pooled into blockbuster accomplishments.

On the other hand, the notes, records, and plaques from committee meetings and proceedings, recording and rewarding and awarding each other afterwards, could fill 500 Libraries of Congress.

The key to a committee's accomplishment, regardless of its array of talent, is usually its **leader.** In most cases a committee of five works best when four don't show up so the leader can just get the job done. Granted many committees do end up with some kind of a result, but it seldom justifies the great expenditure of time involved, all the travel, refreshments, and other costs, all the explanations and reporting. When you see a committee being organized for something and you are on it, do it all yourself the night before and donate the expenses. You'll be time and money ahead.

Meetings

Meetings: when all is said and done, more is always said than done.

Notice in brochures, ads, movies, and on TV how the big-time action so often takes place in a "meeting." The big boss is at the head of a table conducting a meeting. The ad people are assessing the latest advertising campaign for No Sweat deodorant in a meeting. People run things from conference tables in meetings. Not only executives but parents, teachers, and preachers make their power moves in meetings, and crooks even plan their next big heist in meetings. Thus we are primed and persuaded that the best way to handle anything is to "hold a meeting."

This is probably one of the biggest management myths going. Meetings only have a couple of values: to inform or teach a group. But even for this, assembly is not the only or even the best way.

At least eighty percent of meetings are **too long** or unnecessary, and bog down our ability to accomplish instead of helping it. A group converging on a problem doesn't guarantee anything. "Parleys" don't assure production. When people sit down too long or too often to talk, trouble is always on the agenda.

In business or at home, I've found that most people already know before a "meeting" what they've done or haven't done, and what they should do. The main purpose the meeting serves is to discuss the excuses or distribute the blame.

Actual work can rarely be done in a meeting—planning or divvying it up maybe, or gathering ideas for it, but no actual work. Somewhere, sometime, somebody has to go out and do the job.

Isn't it amazing how when we call or visit to get something done, when it's really essential that we get hold of someone, how we buy the line, "Oh, they're in a meeting." It's like meetings are sacred, immune to everyday necessities. The job—getting it done—is the only sacred entity to a go-getter. A meeting is just an appendage of production, so real action schedules and appointments should never be interrupted for a meeting.

Next time you call a meeting watch how much time everyone uses up fitting the meeting in instead of taking care of the problem the meeting is being called for. Can't you just see a mother of eight holding a meeting for every crisis and need in household management?

I wonder what would happen if just before we walked into a meeting (just like when we go to a movie or concert) we had to pay what the meeting really cost us, in both our life's time and cold cash. We'd roll on the floor and kick and groan. Totally worthless "interoffice" business meetings, for example, can easily cost $800-$1000 in wages and snacks, and fly-in meetings, $5000 or more. Often, all for a discussion or assignment which could be better done by phone or in a letter exchange, or someone doing their job right the first time.

"We've got to talk." Fine, do it, but it doesn't have to be in a formal meeting with cookies, coffee, and punch. When someone says "let's meet on it" you don't always need a conference room, an opening and closing speech, handouts, and refreshments!

The more I avoid meetings of any kind, the faster and more effective I get. It's amazing how much less essential a meeting becomes when I say, "Sure, we can have a meeting. How about 6:00 a.m.? I have some time then...." I get a dead silence from salesmen and business associates after that, and they finally stutter and say, "Well, you know, Don, I could just send the material to you...."

Starting today, just for the fun of it, keep track of the actual production result, or gain, from meetings. You'll find so little you'll be surprised, and won't find yourself in so many meetings.

Seminars (and Related Rah-Rah Courses)

I speak with some expertise here, since I'm one of the platoons of productivity experts roaming campuses, convention halls, clubs, and companies, and appearing in commercials. I've taught thousands of seminars, attended hundreds of them, and financed tens of thousands of dollars worth of them for my people to attend. We, like any group of professional "instructors," have our giants of wisdom and our master teachers. We also have our sincere but uninspired practitioners, and our parrots, people who are simply collectors of good production mottoes and stories, presenters of philosophy. And still further down (getting the biggest fee), we have our glittering media-made celebrities, bosom- or muscle-bound folks whose credentials for teaching finance, family management, or how to get more done are questionable but seldom questioned.

Seminars range from life-changing to total lifeless and useless. We've all known plenty of people who take courses and seminars and are no better when they come out than when they went in. About all they gain is a little arm strength, from carrying huge binders of rules and principles back and forth from the classroom to the motel room, where they work on abstract exercises and plans.

Among the thousands of well-sold seminars (from getting rich in real estate to getting a date, from saving your lawn to saving your marriage) out there from $49.95 to $1400 (plus expenses, tapes, etc.), a few are 48-hour clock friendly, a solid help. Many more will just pour molasses in your clock. Selecting according to your direction is the first step in thinning down the choices. Second, pay **attention to who teaches you.** Titles and theories generally aren't the answer, in fact you yourself at times may have more go-getter and producing wisdom than the person you're seeking out.

"Behaviorist," "expert," "Harvard/Yale," "president's staff," "therapist," "counselor," "advisor," "manager," "systemist," "doctor," "PhD," "noted," "celebrated," "certified," "sought after," can all be so much horse manure. Who is the teacher, and is he or she a real doer, or a researcher and collector of other doer's deeds? If he or she IS a master of the thing you're eager to learn, will you get the master, or one of his or her staff members who memorizes a presentation and dishes it out to you for $495 a day? I hate to hand my executives, my children, or myself over to mere polish or piles of projected analysis of never happened. Check the leader out, anyone can write a book, be on TV, or get a degree, these days. It doesn't necessarily qualify them to stand at the head of hundreds and sound off. If he or she personally exemplifies where you want to be—pack up and attend!

Associations, Memberships, Organizations

Bus drivers, teachers, janitors, farmers, fliers, chemists, car restorers, well drillers, computer operators, in fact just about every profession, hobby, and career has an organization or association. We all belong to some, and I've spoken or taught for hundreds of them.

The purpose of most organizations is good and pure. Uniting to pool resources is a great idea, as is having an official place and time to exchange information, upgrade and inspire each other. Well used, groups

and associations promote high production, can enhance the growth and quality of any direction or undertaking.

True to our usual form, however, we humans can and do quickly clutter up and complicate purity. Before you know it, those members are getting together not just to exchange wisdom but to socialize and add members, and then logically there are dues, and of course anything structured needs administration, officers, some kind of government, and a system to distribute material/mail.

Ninety percent of the once-beneficial associations I belong to have become **self-serving, thus self-consuming**. They spend most of their people-power and money organizing the organization, not advancing the goals. May I give you some specifics? I receive magazines, newsletters, and reports from a nationally known associa-

Please send 32¢ in dues to pay for the postage for this request.

tion. One of those reports came three days ago, and only one page of the entire publication was information to help the members and our profession. The rest consisted of time-using, dues-consuming reporting of:

1. Personality and travel of officers

2. Election of officers—lists and pictures of candidates

3. Evaluation of the past, present, and future of the organization

4. Report on activities at board meeting

5. Awards for achievement of officers

6. The President's report (overly personal and poorly done)

7. Thank-yous for awards and notes

8. Pages of pictures of people standing with cocktail glasses in their hands

9. Membership drive graphs/reports

10. A plagiarized poem

11. A survey questionnaire about the association.

If we pulled all of these reports, we would see pages and pages clearly revealing the focus as more on entertainment than education or edification. The same is true of those potentially valuable conferences and conventions. "I have to search for a class or session out of 20 going on to find one that helps me" is a common comment from someone spending four or five days at expensive association convention spots. Here again folks, pure purpose, potential help, but a risky expenditure of time. Watch for the 48-hour clock enhancing organizations and courses; the rest I'd avoid on my road to being a high producer.

PERSONAL COUNSEL (THE FREE KIND)

This is my favorite source of information, evaluation, and instruction. There are a lot of good knowledgeable people out there and surprising as it may be, they are among the most willing and generous when it comes to sharing what they know. Some people are a little critical of "follow the leader" for lessons of life, so they end up **following the followers** instead. When I'm looking for advice I pick a **real performer**, and that by no means has to be a "professional" (who charges) or a professor. If someone checks out, is genuinely productive, proven, and exemplary, what better pattern and pal would you want, and it's generally free. I would learn from a good, successful family before I'd follow and pay a family counselor. I daily seek and get advice from others whose 48-hour watch has a different face and ticks differently than mine. Some are women, some men, some young, some old, some only eighth-grade graduates, but they are experts and they like to be asked. A fourteen-year-old into bikes or bee raising can give you more solid direction, answers, opinions, and demos in an hour of one-on-one than most books or courses could in days or weeks. I've done a number of successful real estate deals, although I know little about the subject. What's my secret? Before I act I go to friends successful in real estate and ask a few questions. I get excellent input on a variety of subjects from many of those who work for me, managers or minimum-wage crew members. I'm approached constantly for counsel myself and give it and love doing it.

Once I identify my expert, I visit with them for a little while till I learn what I need to deal with my problem or do what I have in mind. The person who has not only blazed a trail somewhere you want to go, but gone on to build a highway out of that trail is an especially good source to tap. Big doers are always busy so don't let that deter you. If you can't get to them right off, then just apply:

THE HANG-AROUND LAW

There are some super producers in the world who know how and why and what to do, and just being around them will teach you more in days than you can learn in years from a theory rehasher. They aren't all working for big companies, either—some of the best producers are running little restaurants or stores right in your town or city somewhere. I tried forever, for example, to learn to play the guitar. I read books and plinked and plunked and in two years got "Twinkle, Twinkle Little Star" down (partly). Then a good guitar

player moved in across the street and a couple of times a week I lugged my instrument over there. I hung around and listened and asked, and learned more in two weeks than in the whole two years previous.

If you really want to learn how to accomplish, find a successful homemaker, mother of say six or eight (or even more), and follow her around and watch her for a few days. It will beat any college course in Dynamic Doing 101. She wakes up with a full load and gains forty unexpected add-ons and emergencies in the course of the day, and have you ever seen a break time for that mother? Watch how she does it, by determination and instinct, plus a strong survival drive, fueled by a little love. She never stops or slows down and somehow it all gets done.

So hang around the masters and observe and ask, even work for them free for a while. You'll absorb habits and techniques that will serve you well. You can learn more by watching than by being

EXCUSE ME MA'AM... MIND IF I TAKE A FEW NOTES?

lectured. **Go-getting is easy to show and hard to tell.**

Contact, watch, and work with brilliant "getter doners." Pay attention to how they get ready, aim, and fire. And notice when their house lights come on in the morning and go off at night.

TAKING TOOLS TO TASK

Tools are cool! Tools are the very essence of human accomplishment, our claim to fame in history—their value is almost indescribable. Any one of us without our tools is generally slow and unproductive, if not helpless.

We certainly can enhance our ability to produce by finding and using the right tools. Farmers found tending their fields mighty hard labor until they invented tools to assist them. Surgeons saved more lives as their tools got farther and farther beyond the simple stone knife or the scalpel. Food preparation is certainly faster and easier with the right utensils. You can catch more fish with the right rod. So the old expression "get a bigger hammer" does have merit when it comes to accomplishing many things.

But we must never forget that **tools are tools**—implements, utensils, gear—they don't perform, we do.

Confusing the task with the tool is bad news because nothing ruins a good person faster than getting in the habit of letting failure or success always be the result of a tool. Like the latest cop out: "My computer's down." Anymore, that's like

announcing the end of the world, the cessation of life as we know it—"off line." In other words, the tool is broken, so time stops.

We, not our tools, are what makes things happen.

New trucks (terrific tools) don't help a floundering trucking company if the drivers don't show up for work or can't read a map.

When you're mining, a hydraulic two-story dredge is sure faster and better than a gold pan, but it doesn't matter how much faster and better if you don't find gold.

A wise and well-trained mechanic will benefit from new tools. A poor mechanic won't make an engine run any better with the best wrenches money can buy.

A surgeon who arrives late won't save the life, even with the most modern tools medicine can provide. The Little Leaguer who misses batting practice won't hit home runs just because his dad bought him a $70 bat.

Tools **don't hit and tools don't score!** Tools don't accomplish, either. Tools are only **instruments**.

A tool—something as insignificant as a lunch pail—can make a big difference in your life. By using it to avoid going "out" to eat (solving the problems of interruptions, poor diet, and how to achieve better use of your time) you can have 300 extra hours a year—3000 in ten years, 18,000 hours or more than 2 years of free time in a lifetime—all from a tool! Just remember that the lunch pail didn't do it, your **use** of it did!

Likewise hardware, closet, or stationery organizers don't organize, they're just tools to use. They won't do any sorting on their own, put anything back or away by themselves.

Look, too, at the people trying to manage weight loss. Nearly all of them turn to a tool, equipment, or compound to do the job. All they get is fatter and further out of shape, even with an electronic treadmill right next to the refrigerator.

More errors of judgment are made when machines are involved than anywhere on the purely human side of productivity. If there's a chance that a machine is going to take away some of the work and make the job faster, then we back off and somehow think the machine is going to **do it all.** Machines don't do the work, and they're not responsible, they're just an extension of us—we still have to plan, direct, and enact. Those Dictaphones we all bought a while back to improve our letter writing speed, for instance, didn't help me at all. Mine just lies there in the drawer and looks at me now. Of all the hundreds of businesspeople and others I'm acquainted with, even those in the writing business, I don't know one person who actually uses them. So many of the people "waiting" to write up their life story or family history, for example, believe that if they had a tape recorder or some other tool to make it easy, they'd actually do it. In **all** cases I'm aware of, having that better tool made no or little difference.

The computer is on the scene now, and it's a great tool, but it isn't a partner, an assistant, or self-operating manager—it's a tool, just a better shovel. It can do so many marvelous things, people say. Not so—it doesn't do them, you do.

THIS SHOULD TAKE CARE OF MY OVER-SLEEPING PROBLEM....

THE COMPUTER'S DOWN.

Ahhh the computer, a proven wonder tool to enhance production! The plow, in its day, was of equal value, but not much use without ground to plow. Worthwhile material to feed a computer is like that tillable ground. It's got to be there or the tool is useless.

Once when I was appearing in a "PM Magazine" segment we went to the producer's mother's home to film. She was a writer, and several of her books were in glass cases in the entryway. She showed me her "writing room" and it was one great computer—tables and shelves covered with monitors, printers, hardware, software, spelling correcters, and copy shifters. There was plenty of paper around, too, piles of printouts and manuscripts, and it all looked impressively productive.

She went on for at least an hour about what her processor could do, and summarized it all with: "In these modern times, there is no way to write without using a computer." Then she told me that with the aid of this great machine, she could put out one book every other year, and that

one of her books had now sold a total of 5,000 copies. She couldn't possibly answer all the fan mail (several letters a week) without the computer.

She asked me how my books were doing—I only had three out at the time, but they'd sold 500,000 copies and I sometimes got thirty letters from inquiring fans a day. "How do you handle them? What kind of computer do you have?" she gasped. "I have a 1959 Olympia manual typewriter that I bought for $5, and that's how I answer letters and write books. I can turn out a book every month or so if I want, and I did one in two weeks once."

I have twenty-five books on the market now, and they were all originally typed on old "Oly." This is what the world's most prolific writer, James Michener, uses, too— an old manual typewriter (without a spelling corrector, mind you!).

I own twenty-some computers now through my various companies, and I'm amazed at what they can do, as well as how easily they can actually interfere with production when they aren't used intelligently.

You have to be careful here—many of the tools made to help us do things faster and better, if we're not in control of them, will end up hurting how much we get done. I remember the first time I used an airless spray gun, for example (it can do the work of five painters). That thing was really impressive. It shot out a perfectly even three-foot spread of paint, and kept one guy busy full time just keeping it fed. It saved so much time the five painters all stood around and watched it in awe. So even though I had a tool capable of speeding up the work, more work didn't get done that day. That job ending up taking six people!

Advanced Communications Equipment

A business associate and I were eating lunch at a fried chicken place not long ago, and a fellow strutted in carrying a large obtrusive telephone. While downing two drumsticks and a breast and a great mound of coleslaw, he took two calls and made two calls, all trivial, talking in a booming voice the whole time to inform the whole restaurant of how important and well equipped he was.

I haven't noticed many high producers weighted down with advanced communications equipment—beepers, cellular phones, pagers, etc.—but the rookies sure love it. They don't seem to realize that no matter how quickly or ingeniously contact is made, **the reason for the call still has to be dealt with**. And maybe it should have been done before you got on the road or left home or town.

What a great tool a fax is, likewise, but it isn't a cure for ineptness or inability to get things done on time. It's a tool for quicker turnaround of printed communication. Piles of people cheered and sighed when fax machines were installed in their offices. (Now they could compensate for all their poor planning and lateness.) A poor manager with a fax is going to be an even poorer manager and pollute other people's good work.

I had a TV segment to film one Friday. We set it up weeks in advance, and the show promised to send the final script and directions prior to the show. By Friday morning nothing, so I call. "I faxed it, didn't you get it last night?"

Listen buddy, I don't stand in front of my fax machine waiting for a message to come out. You had two weeks to mail (or even fax) it so I'd have it ahead. Faster may not cure foulups or fix failures, but it'll diagnose them faster. Fast tools actually hurt poor managers because they give them the impression that they're managing, when they're just catching up.

Answering machines: Were wrongly named. They aren't answering machines, they're question collectors. YOU have to, at some later or even more inefficient time, do the answering (or ignoring). I've never liked them, dread the playback, and have found that most of the things on them could have been handled faster, better (and cheaper) with early mail.

Hi! You've reached my answering machine.. Actually it's a misnomer 'Answering Machine', I mean, it doesn't actually 'answer' anything, it's more like a 'question collector', I don't know, maybe like a kooky version of 'JEOPARDY' where you answer the <u>answer</u> with a question, like this one time I remember the category was something like 'ANNOYANCES' and the answer (which is really the question) was 'To talk and talk without really saying anything' and see, the question/answer was 'What is 'rambling'?' I don't know, something like that. So anyway, why did you call?...

Bigger and Better Machines May Not Be the Answer

You might be surprised how much can still be done most efficiently "by hand." One day, for instance, we had **three** post holes to dig on the corral at my ranch. My son said, "Let's use the automatic post hole digger, Dad, it can dig a hole a minute." I told him it would only take ten minutes by hand. "But that's thirty minutes of work," he said. "Yes, but it's faster than the hour it will take to put the digger on the tractor, and then take it off again, so we'll save at least a half hour doing it by hand." You don't always need a new or bigger machine to do more. He never understood that, but I think you do. Sometimes phoning for, waiting for, getting and directing a machine takes longer and costs considerably more.

Another time, a gravel hauler showed up at my place and dumped the twelve yards of gravel I ordered in the middle of the road. He asked me who I was going to get with a loader or tractor to spread it out. Then he left for another load and returned in 45 minutes. When he returned the entire load was spread neatly around, and there was no heavy machinery in sight. Living on and around such equipment all his life, the guy never realized what a single person can do by hand with just a shovel and wheelbarrow.

I hired a construction worker once, Karl, who whenever the job got tough or something was heavy, would stop working, stand with hands on his hips and say, "What we need is a crane." He'd been on government projects where they had a giant budget and six cranes to do one job. Here, we didn't have a crane, nor could we

get one economically. Sure we could rent a crane for $250 an hour and have the job done in ten minutes. But with a little sweat and two hours we could do it by hand for $25.

I HEAR YOU'RE LOOKIN' FOR A CRANE...

Calculators often are the same, if you're just using them for a few simple calculations that could be done by hand in seconds. Toting one around, finding it, uncasing it, and casing it up again just isn't worth it.

Before we got a manure loader on the front end of the tractor, my Dad used to move 12 loads of manure a day, filling one of those big old spreaders full each time by hand, with a pitchfork. He got the job done and was super productive. The new rig could do it faster, but 95% of the year it just sat there, and required a lot of work to maintain it. That maintenance often took more time than the hand work did!

We do this with equipment all the time. Haul in a $175 an hour backhoe to dig a one-hour, $10 hole—because the machine is the **latest** way to do it, modern! (Then we go to the health spa and pay to get some physical exercise to stay in shape.)

How many farmers have gone under after buying ever bigger and better machinery, convinced that it would compensate for production lags or price sags? On the ranch where I grew up we had a little Allis Chalmers all-crop harvest combine worth about $1500 that cut five-foot swaths. It took us a week longer to cut grain with it than the neighbors, who bought equipment that made twelve-foot cuts. They finished up their harvest in two days, and then that $30,000 investment sat the other 363 days. A poor and deadly use of tools.

In my own line of work I run across millions of people who in an effort to make cleaning easier, **overtool**. Under their sinks, in their cleaning closets/cupboards, are arsenals of cleaning potions and paraphernalia that would service the Empire State Building for a month. Yet the house is a mess. More and better tools isn't the answer to everything. Overtooling can easily kill initiative rather than give us more time and ease.

Bigger and better machines don't always buy us time, even if logically and in theory and on paper they're ten times faster than by hand. So be careful when it comes to automating yourself. Automation works well and is productive in a factory because factories do the same thing over and over again—you seldom do. You're a producer, not a production line and there's a lot of difference!

Bigger, better, newer, faster, cheaper, more accurate tools are all time use plusses for you as long as you don't depend on them to **do** your work. You will be out of control when you end up in their hands instead of them in yours. **Think!** A little logic will keep you the taskmaster. An engineer friend pointed out to me one day, for example, as he watched me spade the whole garden in one hour with my shovel: "Don, if you doubled the size of your shovel, you'd do it in a half hour." As technically and mathematically correct as he might be, I couldn't keep lifting the load on that bigger shovel so the job might take three days or forever with a bigger tool.

THIS IS THE XLL 3000! IT HAS A 4,000 LB. PER SQUARE FOOT SUCTION POWER CAPABILITY AND 900 LB. STORAGE CAPACITY...

AT LEAST THAT'S WHAT I'M TOLD... THE SUCKER'S TOO HEAVY TO LUG AROUND!

SOME HIDDEN HELPERS

All high producers, those who accomplish a lot, will have their little pack of hidden helpers, things that aid their time efficiency, help keep their 48-hour clock ticking. These may be very ordinary or quite different from "the norm," but work wonders for them. Some are physical, some more intangible. May I share a few of mine?

1. PEACE WITH PEOPLE

Especially those close to you—your spouse, your family, your everyday companions. You need to be at peace with those around you, because **disharmony is the king of time and energy consumers**. Disharmony takes you nowhere. It keeps you constantly occupied—coping with it, preparing for it, defending yourself against it, recovering from it. Your life companion will be one of the most significant factors in your time usage, your immediate family next, your friends after that—the public affects you very little in comparison. Peace is the most silent, but strongest supporter of doing more.

2. THE UNDERUSED SECRET OF SPARES

I bet one "spare" day a year will end up saving a year of your life, and that's a good trade. By spare day I don't mean a day off or a day to do spare things, I'm talking about a day to line up and put in place some spares, some extras of the things you're most likely to suddenly have a desperate need for. What are some of these spares that could easily save $50 or fifty minutes of hunting and fuming?

Keys! We'd all have traded our souls sometime for just one ninety-five cent extra key. Pens! We've all done more than our share of digging and darting around to find one to capture a note, comment, or phone number... shame! Vacuum bags, bolts, nuts, and screws! Not enough of these (at pennies each) have screwed up lots of our life's time. Basic tools such as pliers and screwdrivers, too, cost very little, and often make all the difference.

What about plain old bread and milk? If I had a dollar for all the times some member of my family has had to leap in the car and speed to the store to get milk because we were almost out, I could have bought a dairy by now.

And oh yes, spare cash. Anyone can have spare cash, even the poorest person. Yet ninety percent of people, rich or poor, do not have any on hand for emergencies or special occasions. Think of the times when even a spare $5 would have shortened a project or gladdened the heart of a child selling cookies.

Think of all the TIME and emotion expended on such things. It almost seems, doesn't it, that we have to meet some predetermined suffering quota before doing something right.

Tomorrow or soon, **hold a spare day.** Here is a little starter list of spares to put in place now, so the next time you're on a roll, you won't have to stop and seek.

keys	pens/pencils
spare cash	typewriter ribbon
grocery staples	toner cartridge
toilet paper	photo film
tissues	scotch tape
paper towels	postage stamps
diapers	scissors
pacifiers	telephone
sanitary products	answering machine
pantyhose	hairpiece
pet food	umbrella
bandaids	batteries of all kinds
gasoline	light bulbs
vacuum bags/belts	watch
flashlight	alarm clock
shoelaces	

prescription eyeglasses
spare tire that works
basic tools such as screwdriver, pliers
remote control for anything that uses one
the smoking material or beverage you can't live without
the makeup you won't be seen without
wrapping paper and bows
birthday and other greeting cards

3. DELIBERATE DUPLICATION

(Well I needed one of those modern executive buzzwords too!)

This takes the "spare" idea one step further.

I have a friend, Virginia, for instance, an elderly widow who accomplishes a lot and is always prepared for things, despite the fact that she has some physical handicaps now. One morning she explained to a group of us at church how she manages this. She needs a cane or crutches to get around, so she can't carry things easily, or go get things she may need. So she leaves a duplicate set of reading material, or the tools to do something she does a lot, in **all the places she's likely to need it**—bedside, couch, table, sun room, etc. Then when she gets there she can just start reading or quilting or whatever. I learned a lot from her and now have four hammers, for instance. One in the house, one in my truck, one in the shop, and one to loan out to kids and community projects. So then when hammering is necessary, I am hammering instead of hunting or setting up. Often the cost of duplicating the often-used is minimal, in dollars and space.

4. INTELLIGENCE GATHERING

In Other Words, Explore Whether It's Been Done Before!

Most high producers not only know, but honor and respect history. Before launching, buying, planning, or paying anything, they will usually ask the simple question, **"Has this been done before?"** A little review then of when, how, and why allows them to become aware of the six mistakes the first doer made, so they can cut a ton of time and trouble from the procedure. I know we do all like to do our own thing, but taking a little time to check into other producer's projects and prowess can give you a leg up on the old clock or calendar.

5. MAKE YOUR WORK-PLACE EVERYPLACE!!!

A high producer never gets to work, arrives at work, or has to look for work—they keep their capacity to work and all their doing power with them. They carry what they want to accomplish, don't leave it on a desk, disk, or in a drawer somewhere. This provides that wonderful aid to production, **availability!** Face it folks,

we aren't sedentary anymore. We are always on the go, every one of us—rich, poor, famous, anonymous, winners, losers, sick, and well. We are moving, always moving, even our children are always rushing from one event to another.

And the workplace has almost gotten too busy to work in, hasn't it? "On the go" means lots of new and different places, and lots of traveling. Time experts now tell us we average five or six years of our life traveling in or on something. Too often, because our body is moving, our brain isn't. Our subconscious may be idealizing and our fantasizer fantasizing—but our doer isn't doing. Many of us visit or listen to tapes, etc., and that to a degree is productive use of travel time, but most things have to be done, not just listened to and talked about and planned for. Again, some of the anti-workers in the world are telling

you to leave your "work" home or behind or at the office. Why? If it rewards you, pays you, educates, interests, teaches you or your children, changes others' lives for the better... why leave it at home?

If you want to use travel time effectively, it's easy—just take and keep your frontlog with you at all times. Having all your ideas and some portable work with you anywhere—work, play, ball games, vacations, church, etc., is perfect for catching the inspiration that floats by sometimes when your mind is at rest or on something entirely different.

Just how you do this can be tailored to yourself. I bring the biggest allowable "under plane seat" size briefcase and some yellow pads, pens, tape, scissors, camera, ear plugs, and a package or two of raisins, and I can write a bestseller or map company strategy 35,000 feet in the air, in a cab, on a fishing stream, in church, in bed, at the table, in front of the TV, on the tractor, in the hospital, at a TV station, or on the beach. The fun begins when your workplace is everyplace!

6. TIME FRAGMENTS

We're always looking for those big nuggets, when the dust or fine grains of gold, saved, collected, and weighed, add up to the same. In fact there are more of them, so in time they'll beat the big nugget. People have gotten rich just saving the gold dust splashed out into the carpets during weighing; I even know of a fellow cleaner who vacuumed up and processed the gold and silver filings out of a dentist's office carpet and made money.

So it is with time. All your blocks or big stretches of time may be spoken for, you may be busy then with other work or family duties, but **what about in between?** The thing we call time fragments. The time during commercials, or when we're riding places, waiting, daydreaming. Overcommitting will teach you a lot about using time fragments. How many of you have been tremendously busy, couldn't work another thing in if your life depended on it, then bang! A big extra job comes up, something you either need for survival or just love to do. You can't slack off your demanding schedule at home, on your job or in the community, or hurry any of the things you already have to do. But when the week is over, you've also completed the extra job and it's well done. Everyone is amazed and asks how you did it, you're Superman or woman, they oooohhh and ahhh. You think about it a minute (you really aren't any tireder, either) and wonder yourself, "Gadfrey, when and how **did** I do that?" You just used the time fragments, the time outs, the breaks, the standing around, waiting, gossiping, and traveling times, and the forty other fragments of time that are available. They're always around and usually unused—those time fragments can bail you out.

The great mistake is doing nothing at all because you could only do a little—enough littles add up to a lot.

Another reason to carry work with you is that you never know when and where dead time will occur. I get five or six letters done a day using time niches. And most of

work). So as we were riding leisurely along, I asked questions and picked up bits and pieces, wrote at night, during meals, while visiting, and even during interviews (commercials take at least two minutes and in that time I could write a good sentence or two). I got most of the little book done that same week, communicated with my office, spread my business cards around and had fun, saw the sights, and shared great meals. When I got home and laid the work out on the office floor, the staff said, "Wow!" Yet I returned rested and really enjoyed the trip. I didn't strain or work hard, I just used the traffic-light time to glean instead of dream, used waiting-in-line time to meditate instead of vegetate.

Thoreau said it best: "What good is immortality, if we cannot use half an hour well here?"

my proposals, promotion ideas, plans, and book manuscripts are done in tiny pockets of time on the go. In fact the majority of the books I've written in recent years have all been done in the little spaces somewhere between my regular ten-hour working day, my family obligations, and my church jobs. And this is not a strain. It's **a break, a relief, and a reward.**

In 1985, for example, I was extra busy: building a new office, doing interviews all over the country, fixing up my farm, speaking to groups—my days were full. My English publisher called and asked if I could come over quickly for a whirlwind week of publicity, meetings, and negotiations in Great Britain. I didn't consider saying no, I just went and completed sixty interviews and appearances throughout England, and finished all the work I would have done if I'd stayed home. Plus on my first day abroad, my publisher had given me a new book idea (on getting men to do the house-

I watch Monday Night Football like some of you, and it always takes 30 minutes to play the last four minutes. That gives me 26 minutes to work and think and write and draw and play with kids, while the game is going on.

How many time niches do you have? Many janitors tell me they have six hours worth of spare minutes during the working day. It's been estimated that the average American spends 2800 hours a year just being a spectator or listener—that's almost one third of the entire year! The Los Angeles Chamber of Commerce pointed out a while ago that over **6 billion dollars** worth of productive time there is lost every year just in traffic jams. And still you say you have no time? Seize the moment and do something with it!

Spare minutes add up. Set a big bucket under a little drip, and when you come back in a few hours, the bucket is full. Impossible? Nope, just an example of the power of fragments. A tiny stream of water can fill a large lake in no time! And even the biggest snowbank is made up of miniature snowflakes that fell down one by one.

7. YOU DON'T HAVE TO DO IT IN PERSON!

Another great timesaving skill is realizing that "in person" is by no means always necessary to accomplish things. There are a few times and occasions when we must be physically present for something, by law, or when something serious might go wrong if we weren't. But you don't always have to appear to make an appearance, I've discovered.

We still seem to have that pioneer instinct to jump on our horse and go, but if you're out for greater productivity avoid it, whenever possible. There is no such thing as a "quick trip to town," and going out doesn't just take time, gas, and energy. Seeing all those sights and people changes your mood and mode and it'll be hard to recapture the rhythm of solitary accomplishment when you return.

One of the most magic words here is "**delivered**." Once I used to go get or run down everything myself. Now I've learned that the little extra charge for room service, for example, saves getting yourself presentable enough to go down to the hotel dining room and eat (and probably having to wait another half hour or more

after you get there, to get waited on). If what you need can't be delivered, see if anyone else is headed that way, who could make a quick stop and pick it up or take care of it for you. Even many "must have your signature" things can be done for you by someone else via Power of Attorney.

I use the **mail** to run most of my errands, and prefer writing to making calls most of the time. Calling is better than going yourself, but there are some cautions here too. One call usually expands into at least two more to check things out further, make sure you have the right person or department, etc. And phoned instructions usually require some written confirmation in the end anyway. So most messages, requests, and assignments I do on paper, and make a copy. Then it's done, clearly recorded and understandable by all.

Checks are another magic tool here, too. I know lots of people who run around for half a day after they get paid, paying bills and settling accounts and then boxing receipts. I run half a dozen businesses and several organizations and I haven't been inside a bank in person for the last ten years, not even once. They send things to be signed and I do the transactions sitting in one place for a few minutes, once!

Check, before you assume you must haul your body there!

8. PIGGYBACKING

This happens naturally if you let it, as follows: While you're actively focusing on and doing one or two things, the answer, opportunity, or solution you need for several others will suddenly appear.

Did those other problems or situations solve themselves? Not really. Your exposure to new skills, ideas, and sources in the course of the tasks you're doing now is what solved them.

This is how active and productive people seem to magically multiply their accomplishments. Some things just happen while you're engaged in others, and that is why you want to keep many projects and objectives with you at all times on your frontlog.

9. THE FORGOTTEN WORKDAYS

There are 52 Saturdays and counting all local, state, and federal and company holidays, about twenty other days a year to be off, to play, to celebrate, etc. You know those "fun days" when most of the world is out killing each other in bars and on highways, crowding elbow to elbow in the malls and fast food stands, standing bumper to bumper in traffic and sunburn to sunburn on beaches. In the endless effort to have more fun, Saturdays and holidays are becoming the "torture days" of the country. By the time they draw to a close, most people have not only spent a lot of money, but exhausted, stressed, abused, and irritated themselves. (But they haven't actually had any fun, so they have to hit it again in the evening to try once more to squeeze out some enjoyment.)

These "off days" are special and hold some big rewards for those willing to use them to do something that really counts in life. Working with and around the family, for example, gives us as much time together as driving through traffic, fighting crowds, and boating around an overcrowded lake with them. But boating is labeled "fun" and "work" is labeled "work," and so we avoid it, missing one of the best sources of personal pleasure. In fact, we probably have more meaningful contact and "one-on-one" time with someone raking the lawn or weeding the garden with them.

Before you get too caught up in that rhythmic little jingle "You deserve a break today," think for a minute of the opportunity to get things done when everyone *else* is out of the way taking a break! I find in business (and often at home too) that Saturdays and holidays are the best days to work and catch up and get way ahead on things. Everyone and his dog is out on the road, or at parks and streams chasing fish and fowl and fighting each other. In the office or your study at home there is peace and quiet and no crowding, the phone seldom rings, few visitors drop in, and man, you can really roll!

Working off days built up my business, gave me a chance to be with the kids when they were out of school, enabled me to get to know my employees better, fix up things around the house, help the neighbors, do church and community work, and even **wash the windows**! When the day was over, I'd tingle with satisfaction (and I'd saved money, energy, dignity, and personal injury, to boot!).

Today Saturday work is almost a curse word, you hardly dare say it out loud—it's an insult, an imposition to even suggest it. But it's one of the hidden power secrets of the producers. Call it the Saturday sacrifice if you must, but try a new angle on fun—work some Saturdays. Get up early and start in on all the things you've been wanting to get done, those "somedays" that have been gnawing at you, that you've been getting nagged about. Do this for a couple of months and watch what happens, not only to your work, but to you, physically and mentally.

Talk about a high! Your Sundays and Mondays will immediately be better, and you'll laugh at all that play you used to pursue so passionately, because the rewards of the work done will be so far superior!

As for holidays, many of us are less impressed than we used to be by them, anyway. We're a little more aware of the fact that these are the times we act silly and eat and drink and buy ourselves to death. It takes a real toll out of the old paycheck as well as the time clock. We hate it before, during, and after.

I still go fishing and go have fun too, but not when the rest of the populace does. Fishing the day after or on Monday you catch more big ones anyway, because scores of fishermen haven't scared them off. And there's no traffic or crowds because everyone else is back to work or in deep recovery. Try working or staying home with the family on holidays or those "big event" days this year on a trial basis and you'll adopt the program forever.

A Productive Vacation?

Sure, vacations are made to get away or get reacquainted, to give us a change, to restore, refresh, and relax us. Playing dead for two weeks won't accomplish any of these. If you can make your work play or fit any of your accomplishment goals into the agenda, go ahead and do something pro-

ductive on vacation. Building something always beats bellying up to idleness, and it's even more fun!

10. NOW LAST AND MOST IMPORTANT: DO RIGHT

No I didn't leave an "it" out ("Do **it** right")—I said Do Right!

Follow the rules, obey the laws, keep the commandments.

Compare high and low producers and you'll find another parallel: righteousness and high production. Actually, it's only reasonable that those who do the right thing most of the time—tell the truth, treat others fairly, take good care of their bodies—are freer from encumbrances such as constantly having to cover up, dodge, and repay, cope with hangovers, fights, feuds, fines, and court appearances. Even the most talented potentially high producers will limit themselves by traveling a crooked moral road. **Trouble takes time and energy to undo**, and then you have to harmonize yourself again with society.

If I had to pick the prime helper of all production... that good old "do what is right" direction would be number one on the list.

P.S. EARLY still gets you the most unsolicited help!

CHAPTER SEVEN

Timepiece Tuners

Here is a short course in 48-hour mechanics, to help you oil and tune your 48-hour clock and keep it running smoothly.

WHAT IS THE OBJECTIVE?

We hear ourselves saying, all too often, after it's all over and it's too late, "Oh, that's what they wanted." By then we've lost more time than we'd like to admit to readying, bringing, or boning up on the wrong thing.

It took me years and some headaches and heartaches to learn to locate the target before I fired off my effort. General direction always creates problems, and somehow we do get through them and get the job done, but with lots of inefficiency, guesses, surprises, and delays. In my personal and business life I get thousands of calls and letters—requests for jobs, appearances, speeches, donations, help, information, and products. Eighty percent of them are not specific, but general requests. I finally learned to call or write back and say "Tell me exactly what you want." If it's a speech they want me to make—who is going to be attending, how many, who will come before and after me, how long do you want me to speak?

It's amazing, how when that accurate and complete information finally arrives, your job is half done.

BE EFFECTIVE, NOT EFFICIENT

While gathering antiques once for my cleaning museum, I came across a well-preserved seventy-year-old gadget with an enthusiastic "It works!" written under the price. It was identified as a "Screen Cleaner," and sure enough, I pushed it across a dusty screen and the little rollers and whiskers and brushes operated perfectly, spinning, rolling, and humming with precise mechanics. But no way would this thing clean a screen which had, as so many of them do, embedded dirt and flyspecks and gnat bodies. It didn't work, it operated. The manufacturer and seller confused movement with improvement.

How often, in pursuit of "doing," are we like that brush. We make motions, noise, turn gears, even raise some dust, but the earth's surface stays the same, as does our progress.

We can be efficient, cover a great deal of ground quickly, neatly, safely, economically, and even artfully, and still do little or nothing.

You can send a cowboy out into the hills on a roundup and he may be on time, ride perfectly, go fast and far, rope unerringly, know his steers and heifers, get saddle blisters on his butt, and sing all the campfire songs in tune—all of this he does very efficiently. BUT... if he doesn't bring back any cattle, it doesn't count.

You can rehearse and put on a stage play efficiently. But if it didn't move the audience, inspire and change them or provide enjoyment, then it wasn't effective. I see lots of writers who have the tools and skills to turn out and organize copy, move paragraphs around perfectly and effi-

ciently. But writing paragraphs that move **people** is the goal—and that's effectiveness. Efficiency is needed to be effective, but it's surely not an end in itself.

CONCENTRATE YOUR TIME WHERE IT COUNTS

The secret of 48-hour achievement lies in maximizing productive time and minimizing nonproductive time. I heard a lifeless talk once that clearly demonstrated what NOT to do here. The young speaker went to great lengths to describe why he'd been asked to talk, and how he'd prepared his speech. He then explained what he would talk about and how he would treat the subject. By this time, 15 minutes of his allotted 25 were gone. He then sparsely covered his topic in 5 minutes. His clincher was a boring summary of the value of his talk to all of us in the audience.

The professional cleaner who gets plenty of jobs and gets them done, but somehow never manages to make a profit, has this same problem. When analyzed, his days have a familiar look.

Preparation and finishup don't pay anything. The revenue earned in productive time (actual doing) has to support and pay for this nonproductive time. Adequate preparation and careful finishup are important, but only in proportion to the value of what is produced.

Your goal is to **concentrate your time in the area where it will yield the most.** If you can manage to do this, you'll continually gain time and multiply your accomplishments. Planning things, lining them up and assigning and adjusting them and getting them started are all important parts of getting things done. But actually spending your time working on them is the big uno, the heart of doing.

PREPARATION
DOING
FINISHING
EXTRA TIME FOR YOU

To give a little example of this here, some officers of my cleaning company had to drive to a nearby city for a business deal. They rounded up the right company car for the trip, some nice tapes to play on the way, called for reservations to eat, checked the weather, coordinated their dress, selected gifts for important contacts, set our departure and arrival times, etc. Little was done for the meeting itself—the purpose of this whole excursion—and it fell flat (but the trip was great!)

BE SURE YOU'RE THRESH-ING, NOT THRASHING

Thousands of years ago now we humans found a way to gain a lot of fine food from few seeds and some work—growing wheat.

When ripe and ready, the wheat was cut and brought to a central location where it was "threshed" by tromping, shaking, and beating, creating lots of dust, chaff, hulls, and straw. Hopefully at the end of the day there was a pile of clean grain, too—the goal. But sometimes the crews showed up on time and willing and eager to work and they tromped, shook, beat, and sifted until they were out of breath. They had piles of straw and hulls, but for some reason no wheat.

This is just as true in our space age society today as it was back then. The mystery of seemingly same efforts with such different results. Let's call the grain-producing process threshing, and the other, thrashing.

Thrashing: when there's lots of movement, but nothing gets moved.

We are all experienced thrashers. One day we hit the workplace and take calls, fill orders, create programs, phone, fax, consult, and at the end of the day we have a

nice pile of "did" and "done" to show for it. The next day, we arrive at the same time, spend just as long, are just as sweaty and loyal, but at the end of the day we can't find a single productive thing done. If this occurs once in a while we can just call it a "bad day." But sometimes that nonmeasurable thrashing seems to triumph over threshing for quite a while. Days have a way of edging into weeks, weeks into months, months into years, and years into a lifetime. I've seen and see good producers fall into thrashing while willing, present, and working. Somehow routines and real wheels are turning in the mill, but missing the grain.

Thrashing and getting paid for it is eventually disastrous, as both boss and employee will soon cease to survive without effective product.

What happens is simple. When we aren't pushed, or pushing ourselves, we add five or ten minutes of trivia onto a call, a letter, a trip, a conversation, a meal, a break, a decision. Say we average thirty tasks/operations a day. Without even noticing it we've used three hundred minutes thrashing— that's five hours! Shaving and adding a tiny bit here and there by the end of the day, add up to a big chunk of time.

Be sure you're threshing, not thrashing.

DON'T BE DECEIVED BY "BUSY"

Busy is almost always perceived as a positive, a word we should respect. We almost always buy "busy." But all it really says is that someone is engaged in something. I've seen busy sleepers, busy timewasters, busy loafers, and busy thieves—"busy" can be engrossed, totally occupied, hard at it, and not helping the cause or accomplishing anything at all. "I'm busy" doesn't say a thing about productivity or value. It only says there is some kind of activity going on. I clipped this congressman's report to his state on his "busyness:"

WORKING WITH YOU FOR IDAHO

If someone were to ask me to list my priorities as your representative, I would put staying in touch with you at the top of the list. Whether it's meeting with sugar beet growers in the Valley or INEL officials in the Falls, I can best represent my district by maintaining close contact. Idahoans want, and clearly deserve, accessibility to their congressional representatives.

Based on this commitment, I would like to give you a brief accounting of my trips to Idaho last year:

—118 days in Second District
—Visited 5 senior centers
—406 hours on planes, in airports
—29 trips to Idaho
—Conducted 6 town meetings
—Visited 10 schools
—Visited 11 weekly newspapers
—Gave 2 graduation speeches
—Attended 7 Courts of Honor
—Presented 9 U.S. flags
—Spoke to 10 Chambers of Commerce
—Met with more than 500 individuals in district

And equally important, I maintained a voting attendance record in the House of Representatives of 96 percent.

All of these visits, meetings, presentations, hours at airports, etc., didn't really say what he'd **done**, or necessarily indicate any worthwhile accomplishment. Attendance isn't an automatic asset.

When you pay out more than a million dollars in payroll every month like I do, you get real focused on results. My employees look at their check to see how much it is. I look at it to see how much they did to get it. Some people do a lot to get theirs, and other people, on the same job, same everything else, don't do a great deal. I pay either way and so of course I'm always looking, teaching, and leading to increase the number of do-a-lotters working for me.

Almost no one sees themselves as dead wood or lesser doers, of course. Many think that if they put on a uniform and show up, that's what counts. Well it doesn't—**doing** does. This isn't only true of the business world, either. It's equally true at home, in a community or church organization, and the most mundane daily personal chores and duties.

A little visual aid may help summarize my point here.

Don't tell me how hard you worked, show me how much you got done!

MENTAL ALERTNESS WILL UP YOUR PRODUCTION

In the early days of my cleaning business, I had two different fellows working for me, one named Barnes and the other named Max. They were about the same age and in many ways seemed similar. No matter where we worked or on what type of job, however, Barnes seemed to get almost twice as much done as Max. The quality of their work was the same, but Barnes was just much faster.

I'd watch them work and there never seemed to be a stride of difference, yet at the end of the day, Max had only achieved about 50 percent of what his fellow worker had. This intrigued me until the day it was all made clear. We were "dry cleaning" the ceiling of a large supermarket. Max, Barnes, and four other guys were lined up on the planks, scaffolds, and ladders all working at full capacity. Max's dry sponge (a special soft rubber sponge used for jobs like this) finally wore out so he jumped off the

---

FOCUS ON THE RESULTS AND FILL IN THE BLANKS

_____ is of no value if _____

Dieting	if you don't lose weight
Rounding up	if you don't bring home any cows
Overhauling it	if it doesn't run afterward
Planting	if nothing grows
Writing	if it doesn't sell, or no one reads it
Making sales calls	if you don't sell anything
Saying "Lord, Lord"	if you don't live right

ladder and walked briskly over to the supply of new dry sponges. He picked one up from the box, removed the wrapper from it, walked briskly back to the ladder, looked around to see where he left off, then began working stroke for stroke again with the rest. A few minutes later Barnes' sponge gave out and he in turn slid down the ladder and walked briskly over to the box and picked up a sponge. But then he UNWRAPPED HIS SPONGE AS HE WALKED BRISKLY BACK TO THE LADDER, and AS HE WAS CLIMBING THE LADDER, HE WAS LOOKING TO SEE WHERE HE'D LEFT OFF. By the time he reached the top of the ladder, he was working. The business of getting another sponge and getting back to work took Barnes 30 seconds and Max 60. Why? Because Max wasn't mentally awake. He didn't think about the next thing he had to do until he was in position, and it was time to do it.

Likewise, at our last company meeting, around a hundred of our managers and their spouses attended. The catering company had set up a nice self-service buffet on tables at each side of a ten-foot hall. The lunch line passed by the first table getting main dishes and baked potatoes and toppings, etc., then reversed by the other table for salads, rolls, desserts, and juice. To speed up the line, which was dragging a little, I took up juice duty, filling and handing each person a cup as they finished filling their plates. I couldn't help noticing that some people went through the line taking about the same things as others, but they did it twice as neat and twice as fast. Others held up the line for at least five minutes, picking and placing and deciding. Since I knew the basic business

efficiency of each of them from their weekly and monthly reports and balance sheets, it began to be almost humorous. Almost without exception the laggers were the low producers in the company, and the ones who whizzed through were the star performers in the profit arena. How did they do it? While waiting at one of the tables, they were already looking over at and deciding about the offerings on the other. The slow ones, on the other hand, just poked and dreamed until they got there, and then faced the decisions of white vs. wheat bread, spinach vs. caesar salad.

I increased my carpentry and building speed 30 percent by learning to be awake when I worked. Before that, I always had trouble locating my tools minutes after I used them. Every time I turned around I was spending ten minutes looking for a pencil or wrench or measuring tape I "just had." My small son was so impressed by this routine that he used to slip in or behind me when I left to answer the phone and hide a tool. Then when I started looking for it he would find it, receiving much praise. It was months before I caught on to him.

The crowning experience, the one that caused a commitment to change, was the day I was behind schedule and knew I had used my hammer but couldn't locate it. I decided it was my wife's fault and went storming into the sewing room to see what she'd done with it. After I made it clear that she'd lost my hammer, she asked me what I had in my hand. There was the hammer... and the epitome of mental laziness.

As a boy back on the ranch, making those long rounds on the tractor, I'd often become hypnotized by the hum of the motor and the warmth of the exhaust on my feet, and mentally go sound asleep. It was always then that disaster struck. I'd hit a rock ledge or an old half-buried stump at full speed, and rip the plow apart.

It's great to daydream and fantasize, but don't let it cloud or crowd you out. You won't believe how much faster you can absorb and accomplish things, and how much less repair work you have to do, if you just stay mentally awake.

TURN IN YOUR HUNTING LICENSE

This seems almost ridiculous to write or to read, but already today I'll bet you too have searched for something for the tenth or hundredth time—wallet, checkbook, rings, watches, keys, stamps, eyeglasses. Not being able to find something we want or need—tools, clothes, papers, addresses, phone numbers, information—turns the next twenty minutes (or half the day) into pure unadulterated nonproduc-

tive time. I know carpenters, for example, excellent fast workers, who lose two hours of the average eight-hour day rummaging and hunting for their tapes, hammers, clamps, etc. Wouldn't you say we spend at least 10 percent of our lives **looking for things?** So if we even reduced this by half we'd be astounded by how much more we could get done. Hunting always undoes us emotionally, too. Unhunting your life is one of the biggest benefits of dejunking—see p. 21. Declutter, get rid of all that stuff you don't want or need (that the things we *do* need get lost in). Then:

1. Have a clearly established parking spot for all your tools and projects.

2. Put them back when you're done with them so they'll be there the next time you need them.

3. Mark/brand them—in BIG letters.

When I was building houses or clearing land, I used to spend about a quarter of my time looking for tools I'd carried off, laid down, leaned up against something, or half buried. (They camouflage themselves very cleverly once on the ground.) Then I got smart. Ten dollars' worth of bright red or yellow paint on the handles gave instant location and identification of all those tools if they were lost, left at the neighbors', or borrowed by someone.

KEEP THINGS CONVENIENT

A young man took a job painting highway stripes. On his first day, he painted ten miles; the second day, five miles; and the third, one mile. On the fourth day, the boss called him in for a talk.

"You're fired!" the boss said. "You were doing fine at first, but now...."

"I can't help it," the young man explained, "each day I get farther from the paint can."

Even if it means rearranging your work station, make sure your key tools, tasks, and people are always **within reach**. Even high producers can be handicapped by long distances.

Laying out your office, shop, kitchen, or yard to reduce the time it takes to process and handle things is an obvious way to increase your productivity. Even simple things like having the wastebasket close by, or lowering a counter or finding a table to fit your height, can make a big difference.

Sometimes we get faster and better only to have the time consumed by poorly located items. We lose speed whenever we lessen convenience. Keep all your active projects, especially, fully accessible. Then even though you're working on one thing, you can easily jump to something else if your mood or priorities change. If the others are open, exposed, in sight at all times, you can contribute to them or pick them up in a minute and run with them.

KEEP YOURSELF AVAILABLE

Notice high producers always seem to be available. Availability can even outdo ability! Yet just when some people are getting their act together, beginning to be real go-getters, they get an unlisted number, a more remote office, three hideouts, and twelve secretaries to screen them off from everyone and everything. Or they go off to do so many things, so often, that no one can ever catch up with them.

No one can bless your life if they don't know that you're alive! Out of work people, for example, who just sit around brooding and reading want ads, cut their chances to almost nothing, because they aren't out working or doing (even free) where they can be observed and discovered.

If you want people to call you, you better not have a busy line, it's that simple. If you really want to do business, then you better put not only your office but your home and your vacation house phone on your business card. If **no one can find you, they won't use you, hire you, or help you.** If you're going to be in business, then be at business, where the clients who are supporting and building you can reach you. If you've asked for customers you've got to be there or quickly findable when the shipments arrive or service calls come.

Yes, I did say earlier that you often have to get away from the mainstream to get something done. But you need to be available, too, on your terms and time. You don't stand in the street or the office with a "see me anytime" sign around your neck. You provide clear and controlled avenues through which those who need or want you can get the message to you quick—and then you can respond according to the value of the person and the event at hand.

QUIT STALLING BEFORE STARTING

A while ago, *Writer's Digest* ran the list on the following page of some of the endless ways would-be writers can find to delay getting on with the job of writing.

CHECKLIST FOR ACTION

You've Already:

changed your t-shirt to a sweatshirt (or your
    sweatshirt to a t-shirt)
put on your house slippers
cleaned your glasses
reset your watch
loosened your belt
trimmed your nails
scratched your head
washed your hands again
studied your profile
checked for grey hairs
washed your face
trimmed your beard
combed your hair
reinspected your wart
plucked your eyebrows
brushed your teeth, put cap back on tube,
    rolled tube up neatly
cleaned your comb and brush
put the paper on the roll
fed the dog
put the cat out
made a snack
looked out the window
ate your snack
checked the fish tank
brought in the milk or mail or paper
put the dishes away
made coffee
poured coffee
spilled coffee
read the cereal box again
weighed yourself
run out for cigarettes
cleaned the light switch
washed the desktop
adjusted the lamp
Windexed your typewriter keys
thinned the Liquid Paper
emptied the wastebasket
chewed your pencil
practiced a new signature
rubbed the rubber cement off your desk
added thinner to the gluepot
put more glue in because it was too thin
changed the typewriter ribbon

aligned and realigned the paper in the
    typewriter
inspected the watermark on the paper
filled the stapler
emptied the ashtray
played with paper clips
picked the paper clips out of the rug
lined up your erasers
gone through your In-box
straightened your papers
sharpened your pencils
emptied the pencil sharpener
called your mother/grandmother/aunt
selected a record or FM station
alphabetized your record collection
put Dewey Decimal numbers on all your
    reference books
done your sit-ups
cleaned your pipe
stood on your head to clear your brain
dusted the top of the bookcase
checked out the late movie on TV
looked through the junk mail
perused the latest L. L. Bean catalog
balanced your checkbook
done last month's expense account
remembered... the cleaners... your niece's
    birthday
made that tune-up appointment
cleaned out your notebook
re-prioritized your old list
typed a new list
straightened the pictures on the wall
emptied your pockets
inspected your wedding ring for wear
leafed through *Writer's Market*
read the captions under the pictures in the
    dictionary
read A to Australia and Walton to Zygote
read a few old *National Geographics*
matched all your socks
put all the hangers in the closet facing the
    same way
checked the oil in the lawn mower
put a fresh box of baking soda in the fridge

THERE'S PROBABLY NOTHING LEFT TO DO BUT WRITE...

If this looks familiar, it's because we are **all** artists at stretching out the start of something, when we want to. We can call this twinking, piddling, or my favorite word for it, dinging, but under any name it is a real timewaster.

If you want to see a quick increase in your productivity, just make sure all your time on a job or project is working time. Most people hunt, muse, head-scratch, daydream, pick up things and put them down again, etc., for at least half of each hour they work.

LEAVE YOURSELF A STARTING PLACE

Even the most disciplined of us sometimes has trouble getting started. So when you have to leave something partly done, and pick it up again later or some other time, always leave an easy starting place. Leave things ready—the bins full, the buckets handy, the clothes laid out on a cold morning, the car filled with gas the night before. Make sure the tools are sharpened, set the dishes out, mark the place in the book so you don't have to search for it, write the number to call by the phone so you can make the call instantly instead of pausing to look things up.

Leave things neat and organized, too. Straightening up a mess at the start might technically take the same time as it would to clean things up the night before, but the mental effort of facing that mess WILL delay the starting, of even the best producer. Sorting things out all over again when you arrive is a real bummer, compared to being able to pick things right up and start making time the minute you get there.

GET MOVING— IT WILL MOTIVATE YOU

A large rock appeared in an excavation project and seemed glued to mother earth. Five people worked on it with crowbars and shovels until they were drained of energy. They lost not only their head of steam, but all desire to even attempt it further—not an ounce of muscle, will, or ambition was left in the lot. Even lighting the fuse on dynamite sounded like too much work. So like most "immovable" tasks, it was tabled until tomorrow.

As they were all wearily picking up their lunch pails and putting on their coats to leave at quitting time, one of the workers, taking one last look, found a little ledge that would serve as perfect fulcrum. He set up a lever and applied a little push, and that massive rock MOVED, just a little. But a movement, any movement, said it could be done and **was** being done! All five flung off their coats and for the next 3 1/2 hours, without a break or a drink of water, they wrestled with that rock until they removed it, and then went home humming and refreshed.

You too have observed this all your life—how mood can speed or stymie a job that needs to be done. The problem is that we wait for our mood to be just right, or until we have the ideal conditions or the perfect convenience, and then go for it. The perfect time for something comes about one time in one hundred, so we drift and wait through the 99 others.

But mood is made by movement. So start. Once you're started you are indeed half done, all producers live that motto. You own your moods and make your convenience—"ideal" is for the most part manufactured, not a gift from nature. Just make a move, or get moving and your mood will change. Waiting for your mood to change so you can change the world is like standing in front of a jar of peaches waiting for the lid to come off so you can partake of them.

USE HOT TIMES FOR HOT PROJECTS

While I was still in college, someone told me that studying in the morning was three times more efficient than at night

after work, or just before you go to bed. I tried it and was flabbergasted. **Thirty minutes in the morning beat three and four hours at night.** I could read and write and memorize more and faster and remember it longer. It was much, much more efficient, meaning it took less time to get the same thing done.

Doing the less taxing mental and physical jobs at night, on the other hand, is actually fun, and winds you down perfectly for bed.

High producers pick and use hot times for hot projects! Don't allow low-fuel jobs to burn any high-fuel time. I'll never file, address envelopes, or read mail or magazines when I'm fresh and keen. High producers do trivial things during trivial times, they never use prime time to trim their cuticles. I bundle up all those little things that require reading or response—letters, forms, questionnaires—and when I hit a time, such as on the plane or waiting in the terminal, when my body has to be there but my mind is free, I do them. Never in prime working hours, or when I'm with my kids or spouse. (I've even been known to discharge a few detail chores during dry sermons....)

SHIP JUMPING

High producers are often asked, Where do you get the energy, the ambition to do all that you do? After all, it's easy enough to get discouraged, bored, tired, and impatient with one project. Well guess what, the go-getters also get discouraged, bored, tired, and impatient—they're human just like you and subject to exactly the same emotions and psychic forces. That's WHY they have multiple things going.

I call this approach "ship jumping," meaning that when a project or task starts to get draggy or uninteresting, I don't have a part or supply that I need to continue, etc., I jump ship, leave it, go do something else. We all do this somewhere. When we're been lying in bed or standing in line, been in the same position too long, and our arms or legs are cramped or gone to sleep, we shift our weight or position, stretch out, curl up, roll over—anything to break the bind, and boy, does it feel good. Or we're carrying a heavy suitcase in one

arm and a pile of gifts in the other, and our arms begin to set up like cement and our muscles start to twitch with pain. Then we just change hands, and have not only relief but renewed strength, and can continue on our way.

We only have so much endurance, mental and physical, for any one task, and jumping ship is a great way to keep going... with others. Just be sure, if you're going to be a ship jumper, that you have a big fleet, so when you leave one ship, you have another to board immediately. Lots of people quit a project, or fail at it, and then just lie around and go stale. Doers quit and leave projects too, probably more than anyone else. Their secret is, they have forty others (fresh, new, and interesting) which they can leap onto. Then an hour, a day, or a week later, when that one gets dull and they begin to get bored, they can jump ship again.

When my wife and I go to Hawaii for two months or so in the winter, everyone assumes that we're just resting up from a

busy and demanding year. When we leave there, however, we've not only made progress on the low-maintenance house we're building there, we've usually accomplished 15 or 20 other major projects and hundreds of minor ones in those two months. Yet we still did rest and enjoy all the exotic sights and sounds.

Hawaii is a place where the body says, "I'm sleepy," or "I'm hungry" often, and there if I had only one or two things or nothing to do, I'd eat and sleep the whole two months away. But eating and sleeping is only so rewarding, so I spend the entire time jumping ship. What ships do I jump? Well, besides planning and building toward that low-upkeep house, I have the four or five new books I'm always working on, plus a pile of other projects to choose from. I'm building a volcano (with a hidden storage building inside) out of lava rock. We're also planting trees and bushes and building a nature trail. I'm making a set of steps down into the jungle, a huge rock and block fence, and a scary "Raiders of the Lost Ark" bridge. And I'm always happy to help the neighbors out when they're painting a house or putting up a garage.

So there are plenty of places to go when I jump ship. I work on the fence when it's cloudy, because that tropical sun shining down on those black rocks could cook you. Instead of fighting it, I go into the shade and plant a tree or two, weed the ferns for an hour or so till I get bored. Then I grab my machete and head for the cool edge of the jungle and hack back the overgrowth for an hour, and when the rains come I go into the house and write on one of my books. When I hit a writer's block, instead of beating my head against it, I shift to another book and let the first one simmer a while. I type, and when my brain waves seem to be starting to waver, I switch over and write by hand. After three hours of intense authorship, instead of forcing myself through three inefficient and uninspired hours more, I switch to something else like clipping and pasting art ideas, doing some layout, designing a new book cover—just keep flowing. When I'm feeling drowsy, I run out to the volcano and heave some of those giant rocks around or form up and pour another step into the jungle, lugging 120-pound buckets of cement around to get the old blood pumping. If it rains again, I go fix tools, or go in and write again, or do an interview or play Santa Claus.

Working this way, you'll be fast, efficient, and motivated, not only refreshed but highly productive, because at all times you can assure **full concentration on and commitment to** what you're doing.

Sometimes when things are flowing, I'll write and type for 6-8 hours without ever getting up. As long as a project is rolling, stick with it. But when you start waning and drifting and getting mushy, don't quit or beat on yourself, jump ship. You'll see lots of different things progress and get done, and be able to really savor them. It sure beats the one-at-a-time routine, and it's amazing how it all adds up. In three months of just random and catch-can working, I've completed 300 feet of trail, 100 feet of fence, 20 feet of the steps, all of a volcano, and written four new books, plus done dozens of media interviews!

Stay aboard only as long as you're enjoying the ride. When you reach the point of stalling out in your production, you'll know it, so change, do something else or just go to bed if you have to, to revitalize yourself.

Can you get more done when you're mad? I doubt it.

Mood affects all productivity—and the worse the mood, the greater the likelihood of bad judgment (even if speed picks up). We can't go around waiting for the perfect mood to complement our agenda or spending tons of time psyching and re-psyching ourselves. Real producers handle the mood liability by having **many projects, jobs, and duties lined up all the time. Then they can simply jump ship to the one where the juices are flowing.** When one thing gets boring or too hard to take, leave it for a while and tackle the one you're in the mood for. Mood swing is real, so fit the job to it instead of the mood to the job.

HOW TO SWITCH SMOOTHLY FROM ONE JOB TO ANOTHER

To avoid any time lost "changing gears" here, do it all in your mind before you actually stop and change what you're doing. An hour or so before you quit pouring concrete and go back to your desk, or before you leave your desk to go pour concrete, make the transition and start organizing and doing the next task slowly in your head. This way you're always in gear and in full swing when you get to your new assignment. You don't have to stand or sit in front of it for fifteen minutes psyching yourself up.

DO IT NOW AND PERFECT IT LATER

Lots of us whine and worry and even punish ourselves when we aren't quite 100 percent pleased with our progress or the outcome of some of our projects. Just remember that none of us can do everything well, and rest easy because all through life you'll find that **expediency generally outdoes perfection.** A savvy advertising executive told me something once that I've found to be true in almost any endeavor. "You can get more accomplished by getting something done, even a little rough, than polishing and procrastinating it indefinitely. Do it the best you can with what you have, and get it out there, where you and others can see and comment on (and criticize) it. You'll reach your goal faster this way than by working forever somewhere off by yourself, stewing away and trying to mold and perfect something by the book, or by the anticipated reaction to it."

No producer ever whimpers about not being very good at something. They may know they aren't, and not even know how or when to do it. But if it has to be done, they launch into it and then melt down the bullets they dodge to redo and rebuild it as they need to. Some of my best stories, scripts, and other accomplishments have been the result of feedback on far-from-perfect trial balloons. Often "rough cut" is the best way to cut time use.

FACING IT IS EASIER THAN FEARING IT

The expression "I'd rather face a firing squad than face that" is almost literally true for us at times. After we've conquered the majority of obstacles to our objective, there are always two or three we've held out till last... those unpleasantries, or even downright nasties. The things we would rather not have anything to do with. Example: The committee appoints us to tell Joe Higgins that the job he has held for 12 years is to be taken by someone else and he is through.

Unpleasantries come along at times of victory as well as defeat and at any time are unwelcome. The strongest of us will draw up into a little ball of nerves at the thought of "that certain unpleasantry." People have resorted to lying, cheating, stealing, defecting, and even suicide to avoid facing something really unpleasant.

Many good businesspeople capable of excellent comprehension, accurate bidding, and efficient job operation have failed because they disliked and avoided a few minutes a day of the unpleasantry of paperwork. Unpleasantries, if you attempt to ignore them, will not only sabotage you but rob you of your mental and physical energies.

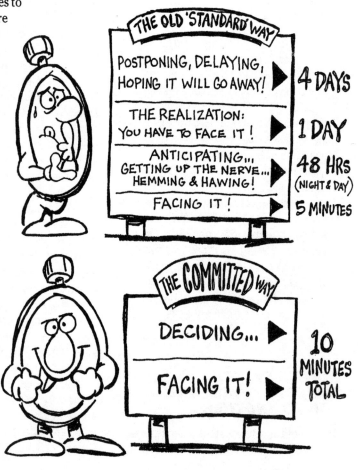

THE OLD 'STANDARD' WAY

POSTPONING, DELAYING, HOPING IT WILL GO AWAY! ▶ 4 DAYS

THE REALIZATION: YOU HAVE TO FACE IT! ▶ 1 DAY

ANTICIPATING... GETTING UP THE NERVE... HEMMING & HAWING! ▶ 48 HRS (NIGHT & DAY)

FACING IT! ▶ 5 MINUTES

THE COMMITTED WAY

DECIDING... ▶

FACING IT! ▶

10 MINUTES TOTAL

When the interstate highway came through our area, it had to come right through the mountains. Even in a situation like this there is some soft going but sooner or later, comes a "thump," **an unpleasantry**—solid rock—and the contractor, like us, has to face it. He can work around those rocks for a while, but before he can go on, they have to be blasted out. The contractor has a commitment, a contract that specifies where the road must go and how. Rocks, if they are encountered, must be removed so the highway can go on.

The contractor can't afford to procrastinate the extraction, he will be penalized, and the same is true of us. He will lose money, and us, precious time. We can easily lose many hours of time and energy dreading, worrying about, postponing, and trying to decide what to do about unpleasantries. The five or fifteen minutes it actually takes to finally face many things will be much less painful than five hours or five days of anticipation agony. Sometimes the agony of anticipation is so long and intense that the unpleasantries never **are** faced, so we suffer guilt for our failure to face them as well as the practical consequences of those undone things.

So what is the secret of facing up to things like this? Direction, again. If you are committed you have no other choice. This eliminates that "getting up the nerve time" and just gets the job done. Your commitment doesn't remove the unpleasantry, it merely forces you to deal with it, do it. Then it generally **is** removed, and the relief and freedom that follows is high octane fuel to boost our future achievements far beyond anything we may have lost in the facing.

HAVE NOTHING AROUND YOU THAT DOESN'T WORK

What's worse than finding the shovel handle split when you feel like digging, trying to start a dead lawn mower when it's time to mow, or limping along with scissors that won't cut? Think of all the things you own right now that won't work. **What good are they, not working?** They have to be fixed sometime and that time always ends up being when you're ready and in the mood and need to use them NOW.

Broken or poorly working things, dull, half-functioning tools always ruin other things including our temperament when we try to use them. They slow us up, and never allow us to be a real go-getter. Fighting a sticky window or drawer over and over isn't very productive, and breaking it while fighting it even less so.

Here's one of the easier high production principles to put in practice: **Don't own anything that doesn't work.** It'll let you down at the worst possible time (it's cold, dark out, you're already late, etc.). The job won't get done, and you'll lose not only the time and dignity you spent fiddling with it, but your train of thought and concentration for hours afterward. This very day or week, repair or **get rid** of anything you have that doesn't work (divorces may take a little longer). If it doesn't work, fix it, change it, clean it, restore it, dump it, sell it, or give it away. It's better to have no jack at all than one that won't work.

If it won't work it not only has no value, but wastes a lot of potentially productive time waiting around and whimpering about it, tinkering with it and trying to fix it. Its potential to malfunction will guarantee you trouble, and it adds ten things to your mind that you don't need.

This fix it or flush it rule isn't just for tools and machines—it's for habits, procedures, bookkeeping systems, promises, and people—anything that doesn't work.

PREVENTIVE MAINTENANCE

"Breakdowns" instantly convert a productive activity into a nonproductive one. The time and money lost usually can't be recovered, and breakdown can mean not only delay but death or injury, too.

One of the best business managers in the country (the person with the best production results in the whole huge Bell Telephone company) looked like just another ordinary Idaho human to me and all his colleagues. Yet he led the national productivity index year after year for the world's largest company. Nothing seemed to go wrong for him, his output was the highest and his expenses the lowest. An impossibility? The motors in his 120-vehicle fleet lasted longer, and they got 20,000 more miles out of their tires than anyone else did. His building maintenance costs were lower, phone installation times and repairs and other costs lower.

How did he do it? What was his secret? "I've learned an art called preventive maintenance. When I or any of my employees have free time, instead of standing around waiting for the next thing to happen, I analyze the age of the products in service, thus determining that in the next year certain items will be worn out. Then while everyone else is waiting for a problem to occur, I promptly change the old piece or product (which I'll have to do anyway). This not only eliminates the later replacement, but also the incoming complaint call, dispatching repairpeople, checking in and checking out."

He serviced, rebuilt, and restored machines, places, and people before they broke at the wrong time.

This man, a smart operator, also consistently won go-kart races (a family hobby). He and his sons had the same cart as all the competitors, but would beat them time after time. The secret again: Preventive maintenance. "How come your cart doesn't sputter and quit once in a while?" others would ask. The answer was easy: During the days and weeks when there wasn't a race, Les and his boys spent a few minutes maintaining things.

A popular piece of advice we hear is, **"Don't fix it if it ain't broke."** That's as silly as saying, "Don't change or replace tires until they blow" (and kill someone, make you late for an appointment, etc.).

We can't predict or foresee the exact moment that a worn belt, frayed piece of wiring, failing motor, cracked tooth, or withering friendship will finally give out. But if things are kept in good repair and maintained ahead, we do have some measure of control and protection against chaos and interruption. Some people may be impressed by how efficiently someone is able to round up all the cows that get out. I'm more impressed by the person who never fails to close the gate, or fix the weak spots in the fence.

Preventive maintenance is a word first for the home, then for human relationships, and then for business if you wish.

HOW TO DEAL WITH DOWN TIME

We can't control traffic or other people's moods, never mind the universe, the government, and all those viruses and twists of fate out there. So no matter how organized or sincere we are, there come times when our driving gear is thrown into neutral.

Waiting in line, for example, can be classed as "down time," as can other little unwelcome events like lost luggage, no-shows at work or appointments, something lost, something breaks down or loses a part, or a sudden attack of illness or depression. Because it generally isn't our fault, most people accept down time. And assume that when it strikes you stop, wait, criticize, daydream, or otherwise just sit there on idle until you can proceed as before. Forty-eight hour day people don't handle down time the same as average folks. They use it well, and NOW. They sure don't wait until it happens and then figure out "something" productive to do until it goes away. They have better plans, and I'm not talking about reading—we all know enough to carry something to read in case we get stuck. These days, the majority of to-dos can be done in down time because so many of them are paperwork, for example.

I've put out twenty-five books in the last thirteen years, and right now I'm working on forty-seven different new ones. The majority of these were conceived and written while I was gaining my million miles with Delta or riding in a car somewhere, or waiting in lobby lines, or for delayed meetings, or while others were in coffee breaks. **Refocusing is an easy thing.** When you're hit with down time you can draw, diagram, write, plan, call, clean, dejunk, fix, exercise, converse, sing, etc. Whether you're stranded, wounded, jailed, or jittery, there are phones everywhere, and we all have pockets, car trunks, and briefcases. You can easily carry paper, pens, books, and other tools right with you at all times to give you a week's worth of things to do on the spot anywhere, if you need it.

How much precious time with your children, or romantic time with your mate, has been sacrificed to something that could easily have been done in a down-time situation? So right now assemble a big pile of "do when I'm derailed" projects and carry them with you. You'll be amazed how much more of your prime time then can be spent for prime things in life.

WHY CLUCKIE, YOU'VE FINALLY DONE IT... ACHIEVED A 48-HOUR DAY!

CHAPTER EIGHT

The Healthy Stretch
(Will It hurt?)

As budget projections, measurements, expectations, and results were being tallied in a great organization, all centered around how much each person and division could be expected to do, one man stood out in the midst of them. He had the most productive and quality operation, the most satisfied customers and by far the most motivated workers, spent the least money, and had the lowest number of failures in all departments. When the others asked him in awe how he did it, he gave a one-sentence answer I will base this chapter on:

"There is only one way to run this operation, overworked and understaffed!"

Heresy! Slander! Subversive!

Was he ruthless and insensitive? He sure wasn't. Remember he was speaking from a strong, proven position—**best work**, **highest profits, happiest people**. Let's see what he was really saying....

Haven't we all said or heard a hundred times:

- "I'm running as fast as I can now."
- "I'm working as hard as I can already."
- "I'm carrying as heavy a load as I can."
- "I'm keeping up with the rest."
- "One person can only do so much!"

Okay, but **HOW** much?

Who is it that sets the gauge or standard for how much we can do? Do we compare ourselves with what others have done or are doing? Statistics? What our boss or parents or teachers ask of us?

Do we calculate how much we can and should do by comparison or contract, or are our production goals geared to our capabilities as they should be? No one in this world is just like you. I think that is the most profound, stimulating, and motivating bit of information ever fed to our brain. No one, out of all the billions of humans, is just like you. In fact, not even close when it comes to thoughts and feelings and abilities. So why would we, do we, always use what others do, or what we're told or assigned, as our measurement of peak performance and production? Our own capacity—mental, physical, emotional, and spiritual—is the only assigner and regulator of how much we can do.

Never measure your potential by what others are doing.

Only **you** know what **you** can really do, that's why **you** bought this book and started reading it. No one is an official go-getter, that's just a label lying around for anyone willing to fulfill what they already know deep in their hearts they can do.

"I'm running as fast as I can" or "I'm carrying as much as I can" doesn't really tell us anything, because most of us have never really tested ourselves hard enough to know how fast or how much that is.

"I'm only one person" is irrelevant, too, because one person—a real producer—can do more than 10,000 others and have 10,000 rewards and blessings for it. If you're really interested in how much you can do, then forget all the facts, figures, and fictions, and those figuring out "fair workloads" and rest ratios, and charts and tables establishing a "norm" for you!

To get a better picture of potential, when you feel you've gotten pretty well peaked in your production on something, go watch a real professional do it—skiing, diving, shingling a roof, gardening, sewing, singing, painting, bricklaying, raising kids, cooking, writing, anything you like or want to do. Go watch a pro and you'll marvel at how fast and well they do it. When that "wow" of admiration shivers through your bones, remember there are always possibilities of doing even **more and better** than what you see. Never envy a champion, an expert, a number 1 in their field, or covet their prowess. Because they are exceptional or awesome at the moment doesn't mean that you are less or bad, only that you have a greater capacity to do than you are presently taking advantage of.

That's the key to being a great producer: realizing, being convinced, that you have almost unlimited ability. Forget the comparisons. They just keep temporary scores in life, provide some fuel for idle conversation. It's the realization and attainment of **your** potential, **your** dreams, desires, ambitions, feelings, that counts.

We've all shot a contemptuous glance at the idiot who reminds us in a loud voice while we're in agony: "NO PAIN, NO GAIN." One fellow I knew said that to his wife in the final hour of childbirth, and it nearly cost him his marriage. Gain doesn't necessarily take or make pain, it only asks us to stretch a little, and do it often. Anything worthwhile puts a little strain and leaves a few stretch marks on us. You don't have to hurt to have a 48-hour day, you have to hustle, lengthen your stride.

"WORKAHOLIC"

We see this label every day and some of us get accused of it regularly. The implication is that you're some kind of hyper weirdo if you wear a 48-hour watch and really love the work you do.

There are armies of "anesthesiologists" out there trying to teach us to slow down and do nothing but relax. I would confidently challenge all these consultants and advisers with the fact that top producers of our society, the workaholics if you will, are actually less neurotic than the average, run-of-the-mill man or woman. All the "workaholics" I know are enthusiastic, well directed, healthy, and mentally and physically energetic. They use less pills and stimulants, can appreciate play and relaxation better, are more generous with their time and money, and more sensitive to social and human needs (and they do some-

thing about them). They're even better lovers than the mainstream of society. You don't hear or see workaholics whimpering and standing around with their hands out for rescue or up for answers. So if you fear that becoming a top producer might move you into the "workaholic" league, rest easy. It would be the best promotion you ever got!

BUT WON'T I BURN OUT?

The modern fear of "overload" or "burn-out" is almost humorous. There might be some "bore outs," "bum outs," or "fade outs," but burn outs? I doubt it. Most people aren't even lit yet, so how can they burn out? How often do we hear a worker or marriage partner say, "I'm just burnt out, I'm ready to quit/change/retire." The problem isn't burnout. Their flame might be out all right, but not from overproducing. More likely starved out for lack of fuel—doing and its rewards.

Burnout has become a respectable label for quitting or slacking off. That magic word is supposed to excuse us from creative laziness, not eating or sleeping wisely, and lack of consistent production. Burn-

out (with some rare exceptions) is ninety percent **cop out.** Most of us who say we've run out of gas have run out of guts. It isn't production or work that burns people out, it's just the opposite. Actual accomplishment doesn't burden and burn you out, it ignites and inspires!

The following was published somewhere a while ago and the "couch potatoes" all copied one to each of their "workaholic" friends. I got several.

SHORTCUTS TO A CORONARY

1. Go to the office evenings, Saturdays, Sundays, and holidays. Personal considerations are secondary.

2. Take your briefcase home evenings and weekends. You can review all your troubles and worries at leisure.

3. Never say NO. Accept all invitations to meetings, banquets, and committees.

4. If you hold night meetings, be in the office early the next morning. This impresses everybody.

5. Don't eat restful, relaxing meals. Always plan a conference for the meal hour, or rush out and "grab a quickie."

6. Regard fishing, hunting, golf, bowling, and gardening as a waste of time and money.

7. Believe it's a poor policy to take all the vacation allowed. Keep in touch with the office daily.

8. If your work calls for traveling, work all day and drive all night to keep the next morning's appointments.

9. At no time delegate responsibility to others. Carry the entire load yourself at all times.

10. **Above all**, after your customers have gone to bed, work on reports and orders.

Me and millions of top producers **do** most of these things and get a kick out of it. (And we aren't the ones having the coronaries.)

How many people do you know who have died from overwork? From overeating, over drinking, over speeding, over smoking, over playing, etc., maybe, but zero from overwork. So you can stop worrying about working yourself to death, especially if you are producing anything, because productivity shapes you up, rather than wears you down. Why do we always blame "work" for what ails us? Most of us are lucky to have a job to get us away from the real beater-downers—**leisure** and **luxury**. Work is a place to heal and rest from the rush to play, eat, sex, spend, drink, and sleep ourselves to death.

Too much to do is usually motivating, because coping with it requires the most intense personal application, loyalty, ingenuity, sacrifice, and service. These requirements stimulate and build, not burn, a person.

How many great athletes, entertainers, or executives burn out when demands are high and they are producing? Few! Their results refuel, revitalize, and rejuvenate them. When we're working at maximum rpm's, when our efforts are in greatest demand, the exact opposite of burnout usually occurs—it's called "regeneration!" Productivity brings life, love, and renewed energy.

DON'T PUSH YOURSELF?

Don't listen to all those people who say "don't push yourself." Most of them don't have any push or production themselves.

During my senior year of college my wife and I were ready to find our dream place. For us that meant something rural, and our search led us to a small sixty-acre farm nestled in a green valley between majestic peaks. It was owned by an old man and his son: The son had severe diabetes and was almost totally dysfunctional now, and the old man, in the aftermath of some other serious disease, was unable to walk. In his younger years he was known for his fine raspberries and strawberries, and had picked this place as the perfect spot for the final fulfillment of his farming. He planted lots of berries, drilled a well, and planned out an elaborate irrigation system. The well turned out to be a dud and failed to produce enough of a flow to fuel the sprinkler lines. By this time he could no longer walk, and yet when we looked at the place the berries were blooming. A neighbor told us how this was possible. "That old man fills a 5-gallon bucket and crawls up and down the rows all day, watering the berries by hand, and smiling."

He sure didn't feel perfect, but he was getting some near-perfect results, as well as a lot of satisfaction and admiration. As I work and run this same place today, sometimes with a sore back or aching foot from arthritis, I'm still inspired by the original owner's example. **Even restriction has a high gear!**

One trip I made to Portland, for example, I will never forget. I felt fine when I got up, spent the morning in my office, had a nice light lunch. Maybe it was the wet Oregon chill, but that evening, when I arrived at the motel, my body warned me—don't eat! By morning I was so nauseous I could barely crawl out of bed. Eureka Company executives, bright-eyed and bushytailed, had me scheduled for six appearances—shows and autographings—at Stokes, one of the world's largest vacuum cleaner dealers. They had to lift my gear into the car and haul me, hunched over and feverish, to the complex. I set up my stage and then went outside and laid down right on the sidewalk, until high-spirited troops of women, arriving for the show, dragged me back inside. It was a nightmare—them laughing and cheering and me writhing around. Surely I was going to throw up right on the front row. After the show the whole audience surged up and I signed dozens of books. I raced to the back room, found a couch, then another show—and crowd—and another. Longtime fans hunted me down right in the back room. No one recognized my near-death status so they all chattered on and on. My only goal in life became getting through that day and back to the motel. That day, and the next day (which was just as bad), finally ended, and a Eureka executive drove me to the next destination, Salem, Oregon. It took forever, between waves of nausea and lurching traffic. By now I was in terrible pain, I could only walk bent sideways, no way I could stand up straight or perform. We arrived at Whitlocks, another bigtime vacuum dealership, where I was the featured celebrity in a 40th anniversary celebration. They'd run a full-page newspaper ad on me, and 73 TV and 115 radio spots. The leading radio station was doing a remote broadcast from there, and the whole shindig was built on me. All agreed I should be hospitalized, but even dying wasn't an option. There were six shows and autographings and three radio broadcasts set up—I performed doubled over, pale, and perspiring, and people laughed, clapped, and cheered. I sold lots of vacuums, met piles of people, and signed stacks of books. Between acts, I'd crawl under a sewing machine table and lie down to keep from throwing up. The day ended just minutes before I did. Then during the sleepless night of suffering that followed, I wrote thirty pages of revisions on an anxiously awaited new book.

At times like this, you have no choice, and it isn't the money, even—it's the commitment and wonderful habit of production that pulls you through.

Production is Often the Best Cure for What Ails Us

I remember a story Mother told us when we were young about a pioneer woman with four small children way out on the plains. She was bitten by a rattlesnake, and there were no 911 numbers or cars or easy ways to make contact with anyone then, and her husband was gone for four months trapping. Knowing that if and when she died, her children would also perish alone out there on the desert, she quickly forced herself, in her acute condition, to make bread, prepare all kinds of foods, and fix up the house so as to assure their survival until their dad got home. She worked feverishly and unmercifully, and instead of dying, she lived through it. The doctors told her later that all the activity and perspiration, etc., had helped rid her body of the poison and saved her—and the kids!

I never knew whether this was a true story or not, but it did a great job of bringing home the point that work is good medicine for most of what ails us. "Down," "tired," and dispirited can be sweated out of you!

We'll often if not always have something wrong with us somewhere. Instead of waiting around to be cured, you can **use production as a cure**, to help make you feel better. Lots of us with a full day planned find ourselves feeling yucky that morning—we have a cold, a headache, we're tired, "out of it," or in some other condition that says "let it go for now." Real producers say, "Nonsense." At least 75% of the time if you just brace, bandage, or bundle up and go to it, you'll find yourself on all cylinders before noon.

No time will ever be picture perfect for production, and so many of our "yucks" are mental, not physical. We all know plenty of professional sick-leave takers; they seldom are producers. The people you know

who "never get sick" do get ailments like all the rest of us, but they'll tell you, "Well, no use lying in bed feeling miserable, I'd just as well be on the job, accomplishing something."

What they forgot to tell you, however, is that they don't really feel that miserable on the job once they start to produce. They feel needed, responsible, see things coming together, and hate to miss anything... and all of this thrusts illness into the background.

Lou Gehrig, one of the greatest producers in baseball, played over 2200 consecutive games without a miss. When x-rayed at his death, he had seventeen broken fingers (some had been broken twice or three times). He'd never said a word. Just having a broken finger is pain galore, just holding it there motionless. Try catching steaming throws from third or throwing a ball with one.

A champion stays in the game and plays on a sprained or twisted ankle, hurt or no hurt. So instead of grin and bear it,

grin and do it. If

you're going to be feeling awful anyway, you might as well be working. **Accomplishment is one of the few things that can take the focus off pain**, it's one of the best remedies for it. And we can usually work and accomplish as well or even better when we're feeling under the weather— whereas attempting to just "enjoy ourselves" or attend some recreational event when we're feeling down and out is a lot harder.

Production isn't a single-position proposition. Because you have some temporary physical handicap—have to lie down, sit,

or be in traction for a while—doesn't mean you can't adapt and do a different job, a different part of the job you were on, or your regular job differently.

BUT IF I WORK TOO HARD I WON'T BE ABLE TO SMELL THE FLOWERS...

Once you're under suspicion of being a workaholic, the famous quote, "take time to smell the flowers" will be presented to you more times and in more ways than you can imagine. Cards, notes, letters, calls, earnest conversations, and even threats will come your way from well-meaning associates, urging you to relax and be sure to savor life before it goes by. But **dedication to duty doesn't have to mean dull**.

Have you noticed that the people who try their hardest to smell all the flowers are often the ones who miss the choicest blooms? Those who actively hunt for adventure have little or none, and those who are forever talking about and seeking relationships, have few.

The best way to absorb the sights, sounds, and scents of life is while covering and cultivating all the ground of production and involvement—**learning, risking, building, doing.** The one who makes it all happen, who plants, grows, and weeds the flowers is the real savorer, not the person who merely views or sniffs them while passing by. The rewards of service, sacrifice, and accomplishment will fill your soul with sweetness no flower could ever muster. The memories of a creation made or a job well done or a life changed for the good will reward and sustain you longer than the finest and most lasting aroma of a rose.

In the middle of one of my life's most grinding schedules, for example, I took forty Boy Scouts to a Jamboree. We passed some of the most beautiful parks full of flowers in the world on the way, and because my nose was busy supervising the boys' activities all the time, no flowers got sniffed by me on that trip. That was years ago now, but the satisfaction of having made some small contribution to those young lives has permeated my being ever since. It delights my soul far more than the finest gardenia ever could.

I've lived in the midst of mountain pines and alfalfa fields, and smelled exotic blossoms from Europe to Alaska, Hawaii to the Arizona desert. I've loved and benefited from it all, but working long and hard to improve yourself and serve others is still sweeter. And it will give you twenty different, lifelong rewards instead of just the pleasure of sniffing the same familiar flower twenty times.

Busy is the best way to smell flowers!

WORK, THE ULTIMATE RECREATION

Have you ever thought of high production as a "rester" and restorer? If you equate doing a lot with getting tired—there may be a secret here that you've been missing all these years. The reason high achievers have lots of energy, can put in unbelievable hours, is because **doing is generally more restful than not doing**. Doing is less stressful than waiting, weighing, dodging, brooding, wondering, wandering. Lounging lights no burners in the human soul, but accomplishment does.

In the early days of our marriage, for example, my wife and I had our hands full. I was getting my cleaning business underway and averaging 10-12 hours daily on the job, and she was finishing up her degree and caring for our six young children. And we were building our first house. After long hard weeks like this, one Saturday morning I was getting things cleaned up around the shop when an unexpected $150 arrived in the mail. I called my wife excitedly and told her—we were really going to enjoy ourselves tonight. A big night out on the town or a party? Not on your life! That would be a bore. By 4:00 p.m. I was on my way home with some cinder blocks, an "I" beam for the door frame, and some cement and lime. (We could only build our home as we could afford to purchase things.) By suppertime we had butterflies thinking about that evening. We were going to have the whole kitchen wall on the house finished. We would get the kids to bed early, set up the lights, mix a batch of mortar, and lay blocks and beams until 2:00 a.m. or so. Fun... out in the beautiful evening air, geese honking, frogs chirruping, nighthawks whipping through the sky, owls calling in the pines, and our own house going up. Were we on a high! And a lot less tired than if we'd sat through a dance or late show or evening of dull conversation.

Producing, doing something worthwhile, is rarely "work." It's usually restful and relaxing because it's so rewarding. **Covering ground may get tiring, but gaining ground isn't!**

If the Martians arrived and our activities weren't labeled work or play, how would they know the difference?

THE BIGGEST SECRET OF ACCOMPLISHMENT: TIME ON THE JOB

I hired an eager college student once who was thrilled with the job, the pay, and the schedule. One week later he came in and quit. What was the reason? In his very words, "Work takes up all the time on the job." "What?" I asked, "I'm not sure I understand you...." "The work I have to do takes up all my time while I'm there." "I still don't understand you, man." "Well, Harry my buddy has a job over at the college plant

and he reads gauges and makes one round every hour, and then he can sit and study and read or watch TV and get paid for the other six. That's the kind of job I have in mind."

This represents not only a trend, but a general attitude today. The result is that we're all spending less and less time actually working and more and more sick-leaving, training, traveling, breaking for coffee, committeeing, unpacking and packing up tools, showering and forty other things **"on company time."** This and this alone is the reason other countries are outproducing us. It's all a simple matter of time on the job. Diving into and hanging with and staying with a job for hours and hours is getting to be so rare, the people that do it shine forth like a second sun! Buddy Holly never wore a watch and friends would ask "How do you know when to stop?" He answered simply "When I'm through."

High accomplishment—seldom is it talent, skill, luck, or equipment, much of it is just **putting in longer hours.** Lots of we adults keep our childhood attention span. We fiddle with something for a few minutes and if the rewards don't start bouncing in, we drop it and then go into hours of analysis. High production comes with serious time on the job. I'm asked hundreds of times a year, "How do you get so much done?" I'd like to say "I'm a magician, I just presto it done," but the main answer is just plain "time on the job." Sitting down at the typewriter at 4:00 a.m. and not getting up until 3:00 in the afternoon, (not even to eat or go to the bathroom) staying down in the field or at the shop or behind the counter. Amazing how much of a time management expert this will make you, just being there doing, working, thinking, and banging things out, swinging the pick and the hammer, wielding the pencil or the mop—how good an organizer you become and how much gets done!

Most accomplishment, doing great things, takes time. We're such an instant society today, of 30-second soups, fast-drying paints, quick oil changes, pushbutton entertainment, etc. We tend to think everything comes in the blink of a Duracell battery—not so! Things are accelerated today, but production takes time. To accomplish you've got to be on the job, hour after hour, day after day, not out to lunch, or constantly on vacation. Time in the trench is what gets the trench dug.

Often you'll ask someone what they did today and they'll tell you about the project they were working on, but for some reason didn't finish. When you total up the time they were actually on this project during an eight-hour span, they really only worked two hours and the other six they were **around**, not in and on the job. They were kind of working out of the corner of their eye, not hitting it head on. There is so much to do, so many attractive and distractive things going on, especially around home, that we can jump from one thing to another very easily, and remain with some so short a time that at the end of the day we really haven't spent any time at all on what we think we worked all day on.

You've got to put in the hours on something to get it done, period. Not just flash back and forth by it.

The chief difference between success and failure lies in the single element of staying power. It takes a long time to get to work and get ready, why not keep at it for twelve hours for a change? I'm not asking you to be a fanatic, just to stretch a little.

ONCE ON A ROLL... ROLL AND ROLL AND DON'T STOP TO EAT A ROLL!

Watch the do-muchers, those with 48-hour a day clocks (and working to invent a 96-hour day clock). They capitalize on the magic of **momentum.**

They know that one of the real secrets of high production, of winning, of genuine go-getting is, once you're really going, making great headway, don't stop. When the spirit is willing, your imagination expanded, creativity pouring out—keep moving. Don't take a break, go to bed, eat, or anything, even if "it's time." Spontaneity is a source of great progress.

When you have things going, in the groove, everything is rolling, then don't stop and bow for applause, just go for it. When you're on the move and things are moving, **don't stop** to read your press or evaluate your progress or look at yourself in the mirror. When things are falling into place, you feel like you could go on forever, DO it whenever you can. There are times to ignore the clock, meals, nags, even tired muscles and just keep going to the end line. Make it a marathon. Meals, breaks, rest sessions, and any other unyieldingly scheduled events are for people who have nothing else to look forward to. If you're scoring, keep scoring, even if you are ahead of "them," "it," or your old record. Notice that when an athletic team gets on a roll, they seem almost unstoppable—even poor teams crush bigger and better teams! Then what does the losing team do to quell their opponent's progress? They call a "**time out**" to let the momentum cool down and most of the time it works perfectly. Remember the movie "The Hustler"? Minnesota Fats (Jackie Gleason) did it to the Hustler (Paul Newman), he broke the roll.

Likewise, people starting to really move on an idea or project will be so proud and impressed with themselves, they take a little time off to celebrate and guess what? They can't get back in the swing of things— it often takes days, or they just plain lose it. We all know that when you're moving something big and heavy, once you get it

started, it becomes easier to move. If you let it stop, getting started up again is murder, takes ten times the effort and energy, and often you never can get it going again.

Breaking the rhythm of music, a horse's run, or any motion will often not just prevent further progress, but the very completion of the deed.

When it feels good go for it... don't stop, look up, or turn around to assess. As Kenny Rogers told us, "You never count your money while you're at the table, there is time enough for counting, when the dealin's done."

When things start going your way, then is the time to turn on the rest of the burners. Never coast or halt or go to bed because you're ahead!

THINK OF PRESSURE AS POSITIVE

Start down a row of workers and ask, "How do you like pressure?" The first one will roll his eyes and grasp his throat, the second one will say, "Stress and *strain*." The third one will duck, the fourth will say, "I hate it." But keep going and suddenly one of them will brighten and say, "I love it!" and they'll mean it.

I'll give you odds that the "love it" one will be the top producer of the bunch!

Pressure is usually thought of as bad or negative these days, but think of it. Pressure means things are moving fast and pushing hard, or something worthwhile is being done: a lawn is being watered or a spectacular geyser going off, something is cooking fast and well in the pressure cooker, or a diamond is being formed deep in the earth. We couldn't get along without blood pressure, tire pressure, and water pressure. Pressure is like a cast on your arm or braces on teeth—we sure don't like them when they're on, but we love what they do for us in the long run!

Pressure might have a "do it or else" ring to it, but we need some of that in our lives. Eighty percent of the negative kind of pressure is caused by us, anyway, not our company, spouse, or school as we always imagine. "Boy, the teacher really has the pressure on me" (the teacher gave you an assignment three weeks ago that you waited until today to start). "The boss sure has the pressure on me" (she expects

you to produce for your pay, and if you haven't been, *you* are the true cause of the pressure). You're in the closing seconds of a ball game, and it all depends on your next hit or shot. The pressure is indeed on, and who caused it? *You* volunteered and signed up for the team and the pressure potential came with the package.

P.S. One of those people in the row of desks above said, "It's okay, if I attack it before it gets to me." She knows the producer's secret! You don't work **under** pressure, you work **with** it! Pressure is a plus if you're in front of it—it pushes you up and on. If you're under it, it pushes you down.

MOVE IT, MAN—SPEED!

So many people seem to believe that if you do something fast or quick, it isn't as good as if it were done slowly. When I used to tell people I could paint their entire house in one day, they'd gasp in horror—it always took them or others a week or so to do it. "How can you do a good job if you do it so fast?" would be the next thing I'd hear. Technically, the faster houses are sanded and primed and painted, the better it is. Lengthening out the job lets moisture into the bare wood and you get weathering, checking, dust, and insect residue between coats. The same is true of many of the projects and assignments we undertake in life—delay only deteriorates the end result or makes the job harder.

Go-getters go. You don't have to dart like a hungry squirrel around tourists, but hop to it. Running, trotting, leaping, jumping, hustling is a virtue. It's impressive to watch, motivating, and good example for onlookers. It's stimulating for you, too,

and above all it gets a lot done. When the TV sells us cars, soap, or pizzas, notice they show them moving fast, working fast, and being delivered fast. Who in this world today wants slowness, in things or people?

"But it takes time to do anything right"—says who? I've seen people clean as fast as a streak of light and their work was perfection, and plodders who took forever to get through an area, and it didn't look much different when they were through. There are thousands and thousands of employees at all levels who are so slow they are dead weight on the job. They may do good work or be good people, they just don't do *enough* work to count for anything.

Don't make the assumption that something done well has to take a long hard time. Things can be done fast **and well.**

Race the clock instead of watching it! I run instead of walk most of the time—it's fun—and notice others often start running then, too! Humans, like horses, have four speeds once you get past stop: walk, trot, gallop, and run. There is a time and place for all of these on most journeys and du-

ties, but if you'll start and pattern your life from the high end (run) down, you'll get a lot more done and be much more successful than if you're always starting from the low end of stop or walk.

There is a woman who does odd jobs and errands for me, she's 45 years old and has always been admired as a doer. I knew that before I hired her, and once she started working for me, I understood why. Once she had the job or the item to be delivered in hand, she ran, and I don't mean that metaphorically, she actually sprinted like a miler when the situation merited it. It seemed strange to see a middle-aged woman moving full speed, and it sometimes embarrassed her husband and children. But everyone who worked with and around her said "Wow"—and gave her more work—mainly because she hit it all on the run.

This might be an extreme case, but hustling is better than ambling or strolling through your assignments. Dashing is more dashing and attractive and healthy... and productive.

DON'T LET WEATHER DECIDE WHETHER

The dashing young man describing his dedication to his sweetheart was raving forth with promises: "I'd swim the widest river to see you, I'd fight dragons and demons, I'd walk through deserts, just to kiss you. I'd climb Mt. Everest every day if you lived there, I'd run through a forest fire to get to you...." By now nearly out of breath with such unbridled affection, the young man started out the gate, turned and said, "See you tomorrow night, Honey, if it doesn't rain!"

Far too many of us play this fellow's game, letting weather or circumstance be the deciding factor on even our most passionate commitments.

Hot, cold, wet, dry, windy, cloudy, in the mood or out of the mood, whatever—if you're going to be a producer, it's irrelevant. A real producer can't wait until it's convenient, or circumstances are just right, before they move or act. If it's cold then wear a coat, if it's record cold then wear two, if it's so cold no human should even consider it, then carry a hot water bottle under three coats, but **do it** if you've planned for it. No one can plan for all the possible weather or circumstance changes, and for sure we are going to hit lots of foul and unfair weather.

If something happens, go for it anyway, be tougher or take another road, but don't let setbacks or rain showers shut you out of a job. There can be a real agony in doing more when you're doing it under adverse or negative conditions, especially when all the slackers aren't out in the storm. But when the sun comes out, you'll be the one on top, and the one enjoying things.

BUT I'M HAVING A BAD DAY!

I was fourteen and it was a great morning. I felt good, had lots to do, and it was well planned. I bounced out of bed to dress, but couldn't find a shirt and one of my shoelaces was broken. I headed out to the barn for an easy ten-minute milking job, and the cow took off and ran to the far end of the north forty. I chased her for forty-five minutes, and lost my new pocketknife in the process—by then I'd missed the school bus. That meant I'd miss two tests, and my brother didn't show up after I called him to bail me out. Then the cow broke the stanchion. In haste now to "catch up," I spilled the three-gallon bucket of milk on the flowers, which alerted every cat around, and they tore up the bed trying to get the milk. It wasn't even eight a.m. yet! Does this sound like one of your days?

About now something more serious happens at times like this. We come to the conclusion this is going to be a bad day. Things are already off stride, behind, and limping. Our momentum isn't just stopped, it's in reverse. We're going in the hole! So we move into a panic mode, begin to rush, hurry, and find out just how true that old saying "haste makes waste" is! It seems everything waited until this important day to get you. Even the toilet overflowed this morning—right after you dropped your contact lens on the way out of the shower.

What do high producers do with bad days? Oh yes, they have them—in fact, more than the regular routiners because big doers have more things lined up and crowded in. So when something goes off the rails, the chain reaction is bigger and nastier! Interruption, breakdowns, stalls, screw-ups, delays, are all part of the picnic of life. What's the best way to deal with them?

First: Don't let what's still ahead be ruined by what's behind. Most "bad days" start out as just one or two setbacks, and it's **we** who end up making more innocent duties go bad. Just because a tire can't be changed easily, we don't have to kick and punch it, injure our hand, dent the car, break the lug wrench, and offend onlookers with our language. Producers never stew or storm more than a couple of seconds.

True, you can't control the elements, or some of the people you have to work with, or some of the situations they create. But you can control yourself. Don't let yourself be undone for the day by a little discord.

Second: Never announce it to everyone: "Hear ye, hear ye, hear ye all... I'm having a really bad day...." This just serves to convince you and others, too. Then they'll help you find more bad news to fulfill the prophecy.

Third: Set the lost, broken, or damaged aside if you can. There is seldom time and space in the preestablished schedule for the time and cost of restoration. If you insist on doing it now, it will break your momentum and affect the whole series of imminent or coming things. It'll throw you off, or onto the wrong foot with all of them, too!

So gather up those broken or scattered parts in a bag and shelve them (and go back and patch things up at a better time).

Fourth: Your frontlog is healing ointment for even the worst wounds. Have a lot of "to dos" handy at all times—not just outlines and schedules, but what you actually need to accomplish those want-tos, ought-tos, and better-dos. Then when a goodly part of today's agenda goes bad, or a big delay or interruption comes, you won't have to just wring your hands. You can tackle one or two new assignments instantly and never miss a beat.

Bad days are perfect ship jumping times (see p. 113), and they can end up better than what you scheduled. The secret is having enough choices to fit any situation.

High producers prepare for a rainy day with big, current project lists. Then if they're dropped to the ground by a bucking horse, or have to lay low to evade a tornado, they can switch to the ground-level stuff on their list.

Those 5-Cylinder Days

Some days we just aren't hitting on all pistons, mentally or physically. We find ourselves sputtering, lunging, jerking, or dragging through the day or week, sometimes even the month. Well lurching along at a broken speed is sure better than just lying down and waiting for a mystic healing of the soul or those stiff muscles. Movement mends most things better than anything I know.

On that big frontlog of yours (that you are carrying everywhere with you) there are plenty of 5-cylinder level jobs and projects—match them up with your current output and you'll progress and accomplish while you're down, almost as much as when you are up!

Body and brain rarely sag at the same time. Learn to bounce when your brain goes dead—dive into a blood-pumping physical duty until your muscles are making refusal motions. Then when the body tires, lie down and think, read, write, plan.

IF YOU HIT A SLUMP...

In the best-planned weeks of mice and men, regardless of market and demand, schedule and priority, there comes to high and low producers alike... **the slump**....

Things get on dead center, all your faculties seem to fizzle out on you, and no matter how hard you flog away at it, you can't do anything right or fast. The more you fight it, the worse it gets. You stomp and snort around and still nothing, your sales go down or your timing is off.

Fear not, even the best hitters and the highest producers have their slumps.

Instead of getting all excited (like a bird that flies into the house and beats itself to death against the windows trying to get out), land somewhere for a minute or two and figure out the lay of the land, refresh yourself on your objectives, and the reasons why this situation might be upon you.

When I get into a slump, I just jump ship (see p. 113). I go to another, easier, more appealing, or urgent project and let the one I've been on sit for a while. It's amazing, when you get away and stay productive in another avenue, how the project left alone for a few hours, months, or even minutes comes back into focus and gives you a firm grabbing place when you get back to it. Switch! That's why it's always good to have lots going on and lots of options and

135

choices. Most high producers do... this is one of the reasons why!

IF YOU FEEL LIKE GIVING UP, YOU'VE ALMOST REACHED THE GOAL

Remember, the give-up point is always just before the accomplishment point. You'll be frozen to the bone by 11:30 if you know quitting time is noon, but if you have to hang in there all day without a break, you won't get cold to the bone till 4:00. It's the same with hunger and thirst. If you know eating time is 1:00 p.m. you gear for it and are famished, starved, ready to sprint to the table at 12:30. If that same morning you know you are going to miss lunch, you'll be a little hungry, but won't let it bother you until later that afternoon. And at 11:00 when you ordinarily would be starting in on starvation, you'll be leaping and shrieking in a picnic soccer game.

If you learn to walk ten miles, you aren't tired till the nine-mile mark. If you are walking five miles, you'll be exhausted at the four-mile mark, and if you're walking three, you'll be dragging at two and a half. **Remember this,** when you're setting goals and listening to your own complaints.

ARE YOU SURE YOU'RE "TOO TIRED"?

In the last hour or two before bed for many years, I convinced myself I was too tired to do anything but flop down and suffer through a night movie or flip through a magazine. Then I started pushing myself a little. When there was zero mental and emotional energy left, I'd say to myself, my mind isn't working on all cylinders, so it would be a waste of time to do anything

demanding or creative, I'd just have to do it over again. I needed a menial task. So I picked one (like filing) and pushed on it.

Often my road trips start at 5 in the morning, and I get underway with only 3 or 4 hours sleep and do filming or personal appearances or radio all day. After 13 hours of grueling mental and physical effort once, I got back to the airport so worn down from lack of sleep that I slurred my words and stumbled on my way in. I had a 5-hour flight to Salt Lake City ahead of me to get home, and surely I could do nothing but sleep (or maybe die) on it. By the time the plane took off I was frozen with fatigue, and tried for thirty minutes to drift off, but those seats and arms pushed at me from the back, the front, and the sides, making any real slumber impossible. So I pulled out a legal pad and some books and notes, and forced myself to start writing. Within minutes two pistons kicked in, and then four more ignited, and by the time we landed I had 20 pages of the best stuff I'd ever done.

Another time, I started work at 4:30 in the morning, and typed and wrote all day until 9 p.m. that night. I stopped just once for the bathroom and a glass of orange juice, and by 9:59 my battery was dry. I was gone, physically and mentally, and the bed was fresh and waiting. Then the phone rang and it was my wife, who'd been on a trip visiting her folks in Phoenix. She was tired and anxious to get home. She said she was leaving now from Salt Lake City and would be home at 12:30. We hadn't seen each other for a week and her voice was soft and sexy as she told me I didn't have to wait up for her. But for twenty years now, she always waited up whenever I'd been gone. I had no choice if I had any honor. I ran downstairs, poured myself a cup of ice cold grape juice, and went back up to the typewriter. Again, in the next two hours came forth material superior to any I'd done in years. I couldn't believe it, and it put me in such a good mood that in the last hour before she was due to arrive I cleaned up the whole house. At 12:30 I showered and was just in bed when she drove in.

As we've all discovered when circumstances suddenly change, "tired" is as much mental as it is physical. Ever seen a tired fisherman when the fish start biting, or a sagging athlete when the play is thickest? A slow-moving mother when a child is in danger? Give me an exhausted person on a Friday afternoon, who is dead on her feet, used up, doubtful if she'll live until 5:00 p.m., and drop her in a slot where suddenly something critical depends 100% on her. At 5:00, you'll see a rousing, restored, still ready to go dynamo!

Don't be afraid of being tired. Lots of wisdom and commitment comes to you when you're dog tired.

You'll recover, and if you've done good hard work to get tired, the sleep that follows will have the best healing power you've ever experienced!

EXPECT SOME WOUNDS WITH THE WOWS

My ten-year-old granddaughter Kristen on productivity... "I know I did a lot today because of the bumps and scratches." What an original measurement.

During the 1988 Jamboree encampment of 32,000 Boy Scouts our single troop (of 38 Scouts) led the entire assemblage in cuts treated at the medical tent. The tally of nicks from busy knives seemed negative until someone toured our camp and saw the unique artistic walking sticks each boy made (and all the others envied). We led the entire encampment in other kinds of woodcarving, too.

The guy who moves the ball the most in the game will get beaten and tackled the most, and the woman who does the most at work is often the target for the flack of the fifty people standing back and being average. You have to carry the ball or go to bat to gain ground or score runs, and there are just more risks in the front seat than the back. Bruises, bumps, scratches, hurt feelings, even injustices are no stranger to high producers. **It's part of the production package.** Any car that's driven gets dents, wounds are part of the price of winning. If you can't accept this, you'll seldom see production.

When you pull closer to the limit, you're going to blow a few tires, burn up a motor or two, might even offend a person or two, but all heals or can be fixed. The pleasure of producing is balm for the worst wounds. Few of those scuffs and scrapes will show or be long remembered, but your accomplishments will—they'll end up standing out and rewarding you and others.

137

For sure the destination is worth the jolts of the journey, so never hold back on doing because it might hurt a little. You'll get an unbelievable payback!

MAKE SURE YOU'RE IN WORKING ORDER

Your lifestyle of course is your own business, however there some are inescapable laws of production and go-getting. The first is: you've got to be **fit** and **there** to get the job done.

It's hard to produce without strength and endurance—the best tools, brain, or organization plan in the world aren't going to make a low-energy person into a high producer. Doing more means putting more sweat and muscle into things, and even if your work is mental, physical vigor makes a difference.

If your health isn't as good as it ought to be, improving it would be one of the first moves I'd make to become a real go-getter. When we feel bad we not only suffer discomfort, we're cheated out of the blessings and rewards of doing a lot. People who become disabled will often tell you the worst thing isn't the pain and or the expense or the treatment, **it's not being able to work and produce.**

If we're unfortunate enough to have a physical problem we can't change, it may put limits on what we can do (although even then we usually have options). But the other 96% of us, who are probably just overweight and underexercised, **can** do something to increase our strength and capability.

I had a friend who always admired my ability to accomplish, as well as the fact that I was still in college athlete condition in my late thirties. Getting to know him better, I found he spent many of his evenings playing cards for three to five hours, downing pizza, pretzels, and beer. This of course put the weight on and so for two hours the next afternoon he would punish himself brutally, running in sweats with weights. He was barely keeping even, and it took him almost five hours a day just to keep even. He may have enjoyed his time in those smoke-filled rooms, but he was paying a big price for it. He had no time to be a go-getter, which he desperately wanted to be.

Poor eating and drinking (and **any** drug) habits zap the life out of you—often permanently. It's hard to be top banana when you feel like a waddling pear.

Society has sold us on the idea that "having fun"—partying all night, drinking gallons of alcohol, feasting on huge greasy dinners, and sitting around in a boat or theater or on a beach— is going to help us live longer and better. Compared to this, work is about the best therapy and menu going!

If you haven't quite had the gumption to lose weight or quit some habits you know aren't doing a thing for you, harness yourself up to a serious workload. This alone will finally force you to start heading your way toward robust health. Having a commitment to do a lot actually helps keeps you well; it's amazing what physical and mental strength you get from doing and accomplishing. For about 75% of our ailments work, good hard work, is the best cure. And when your work is rewarding, snacks and other sideline things won't interest you all that much!

AND LAST BUT NOT LEAST NOW,

THE ABC'S OF THE HEALTHY STRETCH

A. Ten Cows Are Easier to Herd Than a Single Cow

The question most often asked of a go-getter or highly productive person is, "Boy, you sure have a lot of things going. How do you keep track of and take care of them all?"

The answer is one of the single biggest secrets of accomplishment. It may sound crazy but it works perfectly, it's been proven over and over again. Multiple things don't always mean multi effort! Ten cows are much easier to herd than one single cow. A family of children takes less time and is easier to manage than a single kid. The reason is, the others or extras around help take care of the one. Having just one goal, job, project, or activity going is about the most awful and inefficient thing I can think of. Real producers will never let themselves get in that position. They'll start up and have 20 or 30 things going at the same time.

Notice how even when a high producer is buried, almost overwhelmed, with work—**they'll take on another giant project!**

Observers think they're crazy. Mother-in-laws will whine about it, reverends will shake their bony fingers about it, specialists issue columns of warnings, but the go-getter has discovered something they haven't. That extra job is just ammunition to help get all the others done—it never adds work, it only cooperates and accelerates.

You can easily do as much, probably more than most of the go-getters you are envying right now. Thinking that you can only do one thing at a time is like saying you can only have one friend at a time, love one child at a time, etc. You are capable of doing hundreds of things at a time, and it will put a beauty in your life, not a burden.

B. Fish With Five Hooks on the Same Line

I've employed more than 40,000 people since I began my first business, and many of these have been in "the office" where they are blessed with about fifty times the assignments as those in field and floor work.

Secretaries are one of those office workers that really get the brunt of that extra workload. On the surface most of the secretaries we had were about the same— eager, fast-moving, helpful, honest, and loyal. They were all about the same age, too, and had the same amount of education, even their typing and other office skills were pretty much on a par. But some

139

could produce about twice as much the others.

The standout quality these "double doers" had was the ability **to do things on the way.** Whenever they got an assignment like getting lunch or picking up the mail, they would make, on paper or mentally, a pick it up or do it on the way list. Then while going to the bank or whatever, they would route themselves so that on the way there and back, they could stop and get several other things done. This took almost no extra time and saved another single-purpose trip later. Most women are experts at this and the more children, community jobs, or waiting on a disorganized husband or boss they have to do, the better they get at it. They ultimately become much more efficient than those they work for or with.

How many times do we go **right by** something to do? The secret—well it's no secret, let's call it the key—is staying aware of what and when and where, working from a frontlog. The rest is just a matter of reading maps. Making a special trip to do something utterly mundane is a boring chore we can all happily do without.

Doing things on the way—fishing with five hooks on the same line—keeps your brain alive and people impressed with you, and best of all, your productivity up.

Ever watch a good jigsaw puzzle person, or a poor one? The poor one hunts for one piece at a time. The good one focuses on six to ten pieces at a time and thus has a six to ten times better chance to progress.

C. Stay on the Firing Line

Heroes and champions are made in the battle, in the game, on the front line, in fact the firing line. Where there is risk, injury, buffeting about, and opposition, is also the number one producing place.

The American Dream is personal freedom, but being off the firing line isn't having it made, it isn't freedom. Ninety percent of the time, it's just the opposite: personal bondage! We work, scheme, stick our neck out, and sacrifice to achieve financial independence—so we don't have to answer to anyone. What happens when most people attain "it" and are off the firing line?—marriages fail, spirituality lessens, health deteriorates, enthusiasm evaporates, we become less charitable, and our attitudes sour. On teams and staffs, in families and organizations, **the firing line is where everything is happening**. It's where life, knowledge, and action abound, where the seeds of greatness are sown, sprouted, and harvested. When you insulate yourself from the action of the front lines, you cut yourself off from the very things that make you grow and prosper and make you productive.

So step out in front, to the firing line, where you're on the hot seat to produce and perform and be accountable. The good life isn't luxury, it's the ability to produce! Be where you have to answer, speak, give, duck, and deliver!

If we want to prove ourselves, then we have to keep ourselves on the proving grounds; stretched to and even beyond our capacity.

CHAPTER NINE

The Harvest of Having a 48-Hour Day (Every Day!)

"How sweet it is!" —Jackie Gleason

The best salespeople I've ever seen are those who don't ask for your money or even a commitment, they just talk you into taking the product for a no obligation try-out. If the product is good, the selling is over. You want and are willing to pay. If you could leave your old 6-hour, 12-hour, or 24-hour watch with the dealer and wear a 48-hour watch for a day or so, you'd never return for the old one. You wouldn't even ask for a trade-in. Of course if you are sold on doing more and will stretch a little for it, your old watch will transform into a 48-hour one, and you will have all those extra hours plus accessories not on the old models.

Some of those new features:
1. Endless selection of opportunity dial
2. Bonus builder
3. Benefit compounder
4. Leadership hand
5. Energy igniter
6. Help-soliciting beeper
7. Sinbuster switch
8. Greatness gear

Why it will have so many hidden buttons to bless your life, it'll be like one of these new automatic cameras. You'll probably never even be aware of all the wonderful "built-ins" that help give you that "good life" you've been after.

WHERE IS OPPORTUNITY? RIGHT ON THE JOB

When you're about your business, on the job, doing what you're supposed to do and doing it well, it's amazing how many good opportunities come your way.

I see so many people go out and seek their fortune by knocking on doors and making sales pitches, leaving business cards and brochures. That's the hard way to grow and produce. If you're out actually working—painting, washing, cleaning, fixing, weaving, or whittling something—four hundred people will come by and see you, your truck or equipment and your skill. Before long, they'll wonder if and when you can come and do the same for their house or them.

No matter where I am, I find that keeping busy 18 hours a day—either with my own personal or business projects or community or church undertakings—is the best way to relax and rack up rewards. A couple of years ago, staying in our jungle home in Hawaii, I bought some rocks, blocks, and footing cement to build a 300-foot long fence, a handsome rock wall. Working out there in the sun and air, with all the birds and the view, is the most enjoyable experience imaginable. Good exercise, some real accomplishment, and the knowledge that when the fence is finished it will increase our home's value. But there are more rewards than that from being on the job. The fence is along the road and neighbors, tourists, joggers, hunters, horseback riders and the like are constantly going by. That simple fence job, not counting its cash value and the personal enjoyment of just doing it, has so far

yielded: A mason stopping and teaching me some new bricklaying skills, a college curriculum director buying one of my cleaning courses, beautiful people stopping and visiting, people sharing fruit, food, invitations, ideas, and conversation with me—it's amazing.

All of this came **free, extra** as I was working. Had I gone looking for any of it, I wouldn't have found even half as much, half the quality. Being **on the job**—on location and armed, in action—drawing pictures, digging, singing or dancing, just doing whatever you're there to do, will yield some of the most productive results imaginable. At no cost or effort on your part, it'll all come naturally.

Productivity is a natural attention getter! It will work for you.

PRODUCTION ALWAYS BRINGS UNEXPECTED BONUSES

Don't our most vivid experiences come in youth? Sure we still have some great experiences every day at any age, but the impact isn't the same anymore. Relatives were more interesting, apples tasted better, ice cream was more exciting, animals were more loving, songs more memorable, time longer, and distances farther. And everything smelled and felt more stimulating when we were in our youth. I think the reason is that when we were young **we all were high producers**—tried anything, volunteered, took risks, got involved, trusted everyone and everything in every situation and went for it and savored what came of it. That may be why life was so memorable then and not so much now as we age.

One of the youthful experiences I remember best is hunting time, not so much the hunting itself, as the uncles, aunts, cousins, and other guests who would come to hunt. Cary Grant, Bing Crosby, and Gary Cooper even came and hunted on our places! I got to know the habits of the wily pheasants pretty well because when the big people were hunting I was the unarmed "busher," or the guy who would cut through the thickets and flush the birds out for them to shoot. Good bushers hit every pocket hoping for a reward, and generally the more pockets of wheat, willow, and ditch bank you walked through, the more pheasants.

One day I saw big fat rooster pheasant run into a clump of bushes and he didn't come out the other side—a sure chance for a good shot. Uncle Oscar said, "Go in there and get him." And being a good go-getter, I went tromping into the clump and it exploded, pheasants jumped up everywhere, it must have been a national pheasant convention. Thirty or forty pheasants flew out of that single little thicket, while I was just after the **ONE**.

Such is the lesson, the law, the rewards of production—when you're doing one good thing, not even looking or asking for anything else, something extra and unexpected will always appear.

A friend of mine at great effort and expense took up mountain climbing to learn to climb and enjoy it, which he did, but as he mastered the peaks, other talents came forth. He developed muscles, he conquered fear, learned to make quick decisions, and discovered new strengths and sides to his personality. He found new friends and saw new country. Mountain climbing was the thing he went after and got, all the rest were by-products—they just came along with it **free**, no extra effort or planning.

All producing and go-getting does that for you. Most boys join the Scouts for fun—the hikes and the camping. But before they're through, they learn loyalty and honor, how to earn badges and opportunities, and the basics of business. They have a chance to travel, become acquainted with and maybe choose a career, and keep themselves occupied with constructive things, thus out of trouble. In other words, here too one pursuit brings a whole array of benefits in the end.

Another friend was determined to learn to be a good enough dancer to teach it. It took a stretch—six nights of classes and practice a week—to learn and do this, but she did and she was good. And by the time she was done, she'd not only accomplished what she'd set out to do, and enjoyed herself and made a nice living, but had friends throughout the western U.S. She'd also gained a love and understanding of music and met people from other lands and cultures. For the one thing she worked toward, she received **twenty others**, for no extra effort or cost. They just came with the territory of producing.

One morning years ago, while my wife and I were in Hawaii for a brief vacation, we heard a request in church for people to go over to an incapacitated person's place Saturday morning to do the yard work. I got up early that morning (as good go-getters do) and went over with my shovel and pick and jungle knife for a little workout. By noon I ended up with ten special Samoan coconut trees, a stalk of bananas, three new friends, two invitations for dinner and one to go fishing. I also learned some things I didn't know about gardening, got acquainted with some new tools and five new kinds of plants, and got a souvenir map of the Hawaiian Islands (no longer in print). Think of what I'd have missed if I'd just stayed in bed that Saturday morning. From two hours of work, **ten spinoffs**. I couldn't have done better if I'd paid for or planned it!

Those unexpected rewards from high production are what make for a really fun life. The producing itself is a turn-on and enjoyable enough, but when 10 or 12 or even 100 extra things come along with it—generally **free**—and they do—it's like Christmas every day! Those little bonuses are part of the harvest for a go-getter, one more incentive to become a producer of the highest echelon!

There's something so exciting, so rewarding, so motivating about doing more, upping your output and your expectations of yourself. You do more, and it touches more lives, thus enriching yours. It gives life some intensity for a change, and you make dust instead of eating everyone else's.

Don't we all want (secretly or not so secretly) to change our lives and ways of doing things to accomplish this? Well, I've found a shortcut to it—just demand, outline, bite off, commit to, and do **more**—and better. Quit accepting the level someone else has achieved, or the amount some hypothetical formula says you should be able to do. Living a "budgeted" life is about as thrilling as watching paint dry. Bite off a lot, and if you can't chew or digest it all, spit some of it out or even throw it up if you have to, and call the process "practice," not failure. You can pussyfoot around and do five safe, careful things a day with no mistakes or you can stomp and sprint around and do eighty-five things in a day and possibly fail at fifty percent of them. Still, you'll have accomplished thirty-five! And from the fifty percent that failed, you'll have gained some respect, some new relationships, and experience. That's how we learn, and soon you'll be able to do eighty of the eighty-five with no failures!

LESS TIME TO SIN!

Let's look at another side of it. We all spend lots of time fighting off temptation and problems, overeating, over drinking, we get lonesome and bored. We have to diet and exercise to keep our physical self in shape, and constantly discipline ourselves to stay on the ethical straight and narrow, keep honest and upright, control our passions and desires. Hitting these things head on, day after day, is a rather inefficient grinding way to do it. But when you're busy, even overworked a little, going after all those opportunities to produce at work, at home, for church and state and your fellow humans, many of these problems either never confront you or take care of themselves, because **you just don't have time for them anymore.**

Think about it a minute: when you're out there really doing something—interested and challenged and committed—you're not lonely or bored, you forget to eat... the work develops your physical and mental muscles, you don't have time to gossip, almost no time or interest for trouble. It's free and idle time that destroys people's lives.

I met a navy admiral once, a doctor of psychology. Many years ago, while he was in college, he'd worked on one of my cleaning crews. As we renewed our acquaintance I asked him about his work. Most of it, he said, was dealing with breakdowns and problems of the enlistees—drugs, drinking, emotional disturbances, etc. "Why?" I asked, "What is the cause of this?" "That's easy," he said, "the culprit is **'free time.'** There are a lot of slow times, and times with nothing to do but wait in service life, and they can't handle it. This is when most people pick up smoking and

drinking habits and when the effects of those wear off and things haven't changed, they do nonproductive things to pass time—get into drugs, fights, etc. They aren't bad people, just **unbusy!**"

Everything you know, all the wisdom and abilities you have, won't do much to give you a happy life unless you use them to produce. Being a high producer is like having a big savings account, or driving off the top half of the tank. When disappointments and discouragement hit you (and they will), you're on top of the barrel, not at the bottom. So when it happens, you have perspective and the resources to cope and even give strength to others.

Being a go-getter will even help you develop humility. Casper Milquetoast conduct, or sitting around citing scriptures in a low voice, is not humility, or the way to obtain it. People tempered by the fire of fulfilling lots of assignments, always struggling for great accomplishment, are the ones who really learn humility, it's another free by-product of high production. You learn quickly where you really stand. Few are more uppity than the newly rich by accident or inheritance; contrast them to a person who has produced a lot under their own steam. The doers don't have their nose in the air, yet you can be sure they are confident of their ability—confidence and an honest regard for self are unmistakable ingredients of true humility.

EVERYONE HAS A DREAM OF BEING A GREAT LEADER OR TEACHER

But how do we actually go about attaining this? Neither education nor money nor position will insure it—we all know plenty of people with all three who can't even lead their family or the people who work for them. Great leadership to change the lives of others will come through what **you do and do consistently,** not what you know or own. When you develop the habit of doing, lives will be influenced all over the place and you won't even know it's happening.

In 1956 when I lived in Hawaii as a young man, I met a Japanese gentleman named George Kondo. He was a genuine high producer and he liked people, he lived to change lives. How did he do it? For years, he got up early every Sunday morning, went into his huge garden and picked fresh flowers, and sewed them up into leis. Then he took them to church or work with him and if anyone looked neglected or lonesome, George would present them with a lei. If they looked hungry he'd invite them home for dinner, too, even total strangers. He did this, steadily and aggressively, **for 35 years**. When George began to travel around the country later, no matter where he went, he had friends and loved ones—most of them total strangers before that morning they walked into his store or church and received a beautiful garland of flowers from a complete stranger.

Almost forty years later now, as I travel across the country speaking, all I have to do is mention my home in Hawaii, and many, many times people will come up to me afterward and ask "Hey, do you know George Kondo?" They don't know the astronauts, or the governor of Hawaii, or anyone else from the Aloha State, but thousands know George. Now George is in his eighties, bedridden at home, and when my wife and I go to see him as we do several times a year, we almost have to get an appointment. He is (deservingly) drawing caring visitors from all over the world. One of the just rewards of a real doer.

The extra weight of that big watch is worth it.

No one said it any better than Robert Baird, 1855-1916, in his hymn "Improve the Shining Moments":

Improve the Shining Moments

Improve the shining moments;
Don't let them pass you by.
Work while the sun is radiant;
Work, for the night draws nigh.
We cannot bid the sunbeams
To lengthen out their stay,
Nor can we ask the shadow
To ever stay away.
Time flies on wings of lightning;
We cannot call it back.
It comes, then passes forward
Along its onward track.
And if we are not mindful,
The chance will fade away,
For life is quick in passing.
'Tis as a single day.

WHAT WILL HAPPEN WHEN YOU BECOME A GO-GETTER, START PRODUCING MORE?

- You'll be in demand, instead of being demanded of all the time!
- You'll have more time than you ever had. (And to think people try to find extra time by cutting down on what they're doing.)
- From now on, no matter what life serves you up, you can't be cowed or defeated. No matter what happens, you still have worth.
- You'll have joy in the morning (and something to get up for!)

  When you get absorbed in purposeful production, success and happiness, all on their own, will sneak through a door you didn't know you'd left open.
- You'll know, maybe for the first time in your life, that you really matter. If we have any doubts as to whether we count—to our children, spouse, boss, employees, or just in general as a human being—it's a number one source of unhappiness. If we matter and we know it, adversities, setbacks, and discouragements are only temporary inconveniences and slight irritations, which we know we'll overcome.

When people are convinced that they make a difference, they make a difference.

Producers matter, and **knowing that you matter** is the biggest motivator in the world.

Produce!
A lot!
All the time!
Start now!

What would YOU do with a 48-hour day? Share more, serve more, lift yourself, be more selfish or unselfish? Once you have more time you could even waste a little time if you wanted—get out of survival into savoring!

Fill in your 48-hour day fantasies here!

DO YOU KNOW SOME TIME MULTIPLYING MAGIC I'VE MISSED?

As I explained earlier, the people who really know how to produce are those on the front lines of living and doing. What have YOU learned about the best ways to multiply your accomplishments, speed yourself up, overcome obstacles and interruptions? Would you like to share it with me, and the world of other productivity-minded people, in my future books on this subject? Write to me!

Don Aslett
PO Box 700
Pocatello ID 83204

Other Aslett books you won't want to miss...

HOW TO BE #1 WITH YOUR BOSS

There are all kinds of guides to getting a job, but until now, little guidance through the more critical next step: what to do **after** you land one. What **do** bosses really want?

At last, a boss has been willing to speak out, to bypass all the bush-beating and explain, clearly and plainly, what any boss expects of you. How you can make and keep the boss happy, so you can hold any job longer and enjoy it more.

The following are just a few of the many revelations in these pages you can't afford not to be privy to:

"How Do I Really Rate With the Boss?" (a self-test that will answer that burning question); debunking the most popular myths about bosses; how to make sure the boss feels you're worth what you're making; how to fix job problems before they start; how to predict the boss' reaction to almost any situation; the real path to promotion; how bosses look at perks and benefits; on-the-job attitudes that will do you in; the truth about "playing politics"; 49 things (many of them are little ones!) that will make any boss mad; how to ask a boss for a raise, or for anything; what to say—and never say—to bosses; how to guarantee yourself a good reference; even words of wisdom about moving on to that next job.

112 pages of insurance that those paychecks will keep coming! 81 illustrations; $9.95.

THE OFFICE CLUTTER CURE

If you're surrounded by piles and stacks of paper, haven't seen the top of your desk in years, or you're afraid to even look into your file cabinets, this is the book for you! It takes a hard (but hilarious) look at the state of our offices and cubicles, and serves up at least two dozen convincing reasons to clear all that clutter out (vividly details all the obvious and hidden ways office clutter is hurting us). Then it outlines the cure, including how to deal with those big bad backlogs of paper, how to clear out filing cabinet clutter and turn "the files" from graveyard into a genuinely useful tool, how to set up paper processing systems that aren't just dead ends, how to get control of the mail, how to reclaim your desk, how to make better use of briefcases, and bulletin boards, how to halt the flow of clutter into your office, how to cope with office common area clutter, some easy places to start your office decluttering, even a look at that insidious mental clutter hovering over the office, how to keep your office looking sharp, and how to design clutter out!

192 pages; 186 illustrations; $9.99.

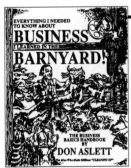

EVERYTHING I NEEDED TO KNOW ABOUT BUSINESS I LEARNED IN THE BARNYARD

How to succeed in business—we all want to know. We've plowed through all kinds of heavy serious volumes and sat through many an endless class and seminar, to find out. Now here's a book that promises to make it all much, much easier. And fun, too.

Everything I Needed to Know About Business I Learned in the Barnyard was born out of Don's desire to "write a better book on business, one so simple anyone could understand it, whether they were running their first lemonade stand on the corner, or going for their MBA. I wanted to boil it all down to the secrets, the real basics, of business. And where did I learn them? In the corral and the pasture, the pigpen and the milk parlor—growing up on a ranch in Idaho."

In this down to earth, humorously illustrated book, full of the flavor of the American farm, you too will learn a world of business wisdom from "the horse's mouth." All those important subjects like buying and selling, growth, inventory, leadership, ethics, business planning, positioning, timing, troubleshooting, time management, personnel management, and equipping and maintaining a business are handled in a way that is illuminating, entertaining, and unforgettable. You'll love it, and learn all the while.

128 pages; 123 illustrations; $9.95.

SPEAK UP!

If you'd rather face a firing squad than an audience, this is the book for you. In these pages Don will guide you every step of the way, answer your every question, and give you the know-how and confidence you need to leave audiences begging for more. Every bit of advice in this book has been tried, tested, and proven in the crucible of Don's more than 5,000 public appearances all over the world.

Just a few of the topics inside:
- The right way to answer that question: But what should I talk about?
- How to ready your**self** for speaking—everything from your clothes and accessories to your mental state.
- The worst fears of the speaker—and how to overcome them.
- How to seduce an audience, and **keep** them under your control.
- How to make effective use of props and visuals.
- How to handle awkward and unexpected situations during a speech.
- The ins and outs of intros and announcements.
- How to handle all kinds of special and difficult situations, from speaking outdoors to speaking at weddings and funerals, Q & A sessions, workshops and panels, debates.
- Speaking on radio and TV (from a real master of the art).
- How to move into the world of professional speechmaking, if you wish.

136 pages; 65 illustrations; $9.95.

NEW ➡

GET TWICE AS MUCH DONE AS YOU DO NOW!
HOW TO HAVE A 48-HOUR DAY
DON ASLETT

DON ASLETT'S **CLUTTER FREE!** Finally & Forever
Including true confessions & solutions from 100's of your fellow packrats.

HOW TO HANDLE 1,000 THINGS AT ONCE
A Fun Guide to Mastering Home & Personal Management
DON ASLETT
Author of HOW TO HAVE A 48-HOUR DAY & CLUTTER'S LAST STAND

COMING SOON ⬅

CLEANING!:

Don Aslett
America's No. 1 Cleaning Expert
OVER 1/2 MILLION COPIES SOLD
Is There Life After Housework?

Don Aslett's **CLEAN IN A MINUTE**

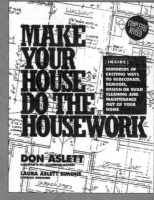

MAKE YOUR HOUSE DO THE HOUSEWORK
INSIDE: HUNDREDS OF EXCITING WAYS TO REDECORATE, REMODEL, DESIGN OR BUILD CLEANING AND MAINTENANCE OUT OF YOUR HOME
DON ASLETT
AMERICA'S #1 CLEANING EXPERT
LAURA ASLETT SIMONS
INTERIOR DESIGNER

CLUTTER:

CLUTTER'S LAST STAND
by Don Aslett
America's #1 Cleaning Expert
It's time to De-Junk your life!

THE OFFICE CLUTTER CURE
How to get out from under it all!
DON ASLETT
AMERICA'S #1 DEJUNKER

HOW TO CLEAN UP, CLEAR OUT, AND DEJUNK YOUR LIFE FOREVER!
NOT FOR PACKRATS ONLY
DON ASLETT
Author of HOW DO I CLEAN THE MOOSEHEAD! and CLUTTER'S LAST STAND

MOTIVATION & BUSINESS:

How to be #1 with your Boss
How to keep your job longer & enjoy it more.
DON ASLETT

EVERYTHING I NEEDED TO KNOW ABOUT **BUSINESS** I LEARNED IN THE **BARNYARD!**
THE BUSINESS BASICS HANDBOOK BY **DON ASLETT**
The Man Who Made Millions "CLEANING UP"

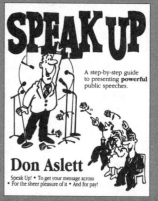

SPEAK UP
A step-by-step guide to presenting **powerful** public speeches.
Don Aslett
Speak Up! • To get your message across • For the sheer pleasure of it • And for pay!

ORDER FORM

TITLE	Retail	Qty	Amt
Clean In A Minute	$5.00		
Clutter Free! Finally & Forever	$12.99		
Clutter's Last Stand	$11.99		
Everything I Needed to Know...Barnyard	$9.95		
How to Be #1 With Your Boss	$9.99		
How to Handle 1,000 Things at Once	$12.99	Coming soon!	
How to Have a 48-Hour Day	$12.99		
Is There Life After Housework?	$10.99		
Make Your House Do the Housework	$14.99		
Not For Packrats Only	$11.95		
Speak Up	$12.99		
The Office Clutter Cure	$9.99		

Shipping: $3 for first item plus 75¢ for each additional item.	Subtotal	
	Idaho res. add 5% Sales Tax	
	Shipping	
	TOTAL	

☐ Check Enclosed ☐ Visa ☐ MasterCard ☐ Discover ☐ American Express

Card No. _____

Exp Date _____

Signature X _____

Ship to:
Your Name _____

Street Address _____

_____

City ST Zip _____

Phone _____

Comments or questions? _____

_____
_____
_____
_____
_____
_____
_____

☐ Don, please send me a **complete** list of all your books and videos on motivation, cleaning, decluttering, and starting my own business.

☐ Don, please put my name and the following friends of mine on your mailing list for the ***Clean Report*** bulletin and catalog.

Name _____

Street Address _____

_____

City ST Zip _____

Name _____

Street Address _____

_____

City ST Zip _____

Name _____

Street Address _____

_____

City ST Zip _____

Mail your order to:
Don Aslett
PO Box 700
Pocatello ID 83204

Phone orders call:
208-232-3535

NEW

GET TWICE AS MUCH DONE AS YOU DO NOW!

HOW TO HAVE A 48-HOUR DAY

DON ASLETT

DON ASLETT'S CLUTTER FREE!

Finally & Forever

Including true confessions & solutions from 100's of your fellow packrats.

COMING SOON

HOW TO HANDLE 1,000 THINGS AT ONCE

A Fun Guide to Mastering Home & Personal Management

DON ASLETT

Author of HOW TO HAVE A 48-HOUR DAY & CLUTTER'S LAST STAND

CLEANING:

Don Aslett

America's No. 1 Cleaning Expert

OVER 1/2 MILLION COPIES SOLD — ANNIVERSARY 10

Is There Life After Housework?

Don Aslett's CLEAN IN A MINUTE

COMPLETELY REVISED

MAKE YOUR HOUSE DO THE HOUSEWORK

INSIDE HUNDREDS OF EXCITING WAYS TO REDECORATE, REMODEL, DESIGN OR BUILD CLEANING AND MAINTENANCE OUT OF YOUR HOME

DON ASLETT
AMERICA'S #1 CLEANING EXPERT

LAURA ASLETT SIMONS
INTERIOR DESIGNER

CLUTTER:

CLUTTER'S LAST STAND

by Don Aslett
America's #1 Cleaning Expert

It's time to De-Junk your life!

THE OFFICE CLUTTER CURE

How to get out from under it all!

DON ASLETT
AMERICA'S #1 DEJUNKER

HOW TO CLEAN UP, CLEAR OUT, AND DEJUNK YOUR LIFE FOREVER!

NOT FOR PACKRATS ONLY

DON ASLETT
Author of HOW DO I CLEAN THE MOOSEHEAD! and CLUTTER'S LAST STAND

MOTIVATION & BUSINESS:

How to be #1 with your Boss

How to keep your job longer & enjoy it more.

DON ASLETT

EVERYTHING I NEEDED TO KNOW ABOUT

BUSINESS I LEARNED IN THE BARNYARD!

THE BUSINESS BASICS HANDBOOK BY

DON ASLETT
The Man Who Made Millions "CLEANING UP"

SPEAK UP

*A step-by-step guide to presenting **powerful** public speeches.*

Don Aslett

Speak Up! • To get your message across • For the sheer pleasure of it • And for pay!

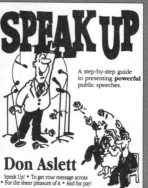

ORDER FORM

TITLE	Retail	Qty	Amt
Clean In A Minute	$5.00		
Clutter Free! Finally & Forever	$12.99		
Clutter's Last Stand	$11.99		
Everything I Needed to Know...Barnyard	$9.95		
How to Be #1 With Your Boss	$9.99		
How to Handle 1,000 Things at Once	$12.99	Coming soon!	
How to Have a 48-Hour Day	$12.99		
Is There Life After Housework?	$10.99		
Make Your House Do the Housework	$14.99		
Not For Packrats Only	$11.95		
Speak Up	$12.99		
The Office Clutter Cure	$9.99		

Shipping: $3 for first item plus 75¢ for each additional item.	Subtotal	
	Idaho res. add 5% Sales Tax	
	Shipping	
	TOTAL	

☐ Check Enclosed ☐ Visa ☐ MasterCard ☐ Discover ☐ American Express

Card No. _____

Exp Date _____

Signature X _____

Ship to:
Your Name _____

Street Address _____

_____

City ST Zip _____

Phone _____

☐ Don, please send me a **complete** list of all your books and videos on motivation, cleaning, decluttering, and starting my own business.

☐ Don, please put my name and the following friends of mine on your mailing list for the **Clean Report** bulletin and catalog.

Name _____

Street Address _____

_____

City ST Zip _____

Name _____

Street Address _____

_____

City ST Zip _____

Name _____

Street Address _____

_____

City ST Zip _____

Mail your order to:
   Don Aslett
   PO Box 700
   Pocatello ID 83204

Phone orders call:
   208-232-3535

Comments or questions? _____

_____

_____

_____

_____

_____

_____

_____

NEW

COMING SOON

CLEANING!:

CLUTTER:

MOTIVATION & BUSINESS:

HOW TO HAVE A 48-HOUR DAY

GET TWICE AS MUCH DONE AS YOU DO NOW!

DON ASLETT

DON ASLETT'S CLUTTER FREE!

Finally & Forever

Including true confessions & solutions from 100's of your fellow packrats.

HOW TO HANDLE 1,000 THINGS AT ONCE

A Fun Guide to Mastering Home & Personal Management

DON ASLETT

Author of HOW TO HAVE A 48-HOUR DAY & CLUTTER'S LAST STAND

Don Aslett

America's No. 1 Cleaning Expert

Is There Life After Housework?

OVER 1.3 MILLION COPIES SOLD

10 ANNIVERSARY

Don Aslett's CLEAN IN A MINUTE

MAKE YOUR HOUSE DO THE HOUSEWORK

COMPLETELY REVISED

INSIDE
HUNDREDS OF EXCITING WAYS TO REDECORATE, REMODEL, DESIGN OR BUILD CLEANING AND MAINTENANCE OUT OF YOUR HOME

DON ASLETT
AMERICA'S #1 CLEANING EXPERT

LAURA ASLETT SIMONS
INTERIOR DESIGNER

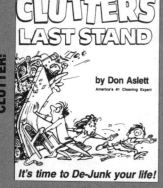

CLUTTER'S LAST STAND

by Don Aslett
America's #1 Cleaning Expert

It's time to De-Junk your life!

THE OFFICE CLUTTER CURE

How to get out from under it all!

DON ASLETT
AMERICA'S #1 DEJUNKER

HOW TO CLEAN UP, CLEAR OUT, AND DEJUNK YOUR LIFE FOREVER!

NOT FOR PACKRATS ONLY

DON ASLETT
Author of HOW DO I CLEAN THE MOOSEHEAD? and CLUTTER'S LAST STAND

How to be #1 with your Boss

How to keep your job longer & enjoy it more.

DON ASLETT

EVERYTHING I NEEDED TO KNOW ABOUT **BUSINESS** I LEARNED IN THE **BARNYARD!**

THE BUSINESS BASICS HANDBOOK BY **DON ASLETT**

The Man Who Made Millions "CLEANING UP"

SPEAK UP

A step-by-step guide to presenting **powerful** public speeches.

Don Aslett

Speak Up! • To get your message across • For the sheer pleasure of it • And for pay!